EMPLOYMENT

Give Your Company a Fighting Chance

An HR Guide to Understanding and Preventing Workplace Violence

MARIA GRECO DANAHER

Society for Human Resource Management
Alexandria, Virginia
www.shrm.org

Strategic Human Resource Management India
Mumbai, India
www.shrmindia.org

Society for Human Resource Management
Haidian District Beijing, China
www.shrm.org/cn

Founded in 1948, the Society for Human Resource Management (SHRM) is the world's largest HR membership organization devoted to human resource management. Representing more than 275,000 members in over 160 countries, the Society is the leading provider of resources to serve the needs of HR professionals and advance the professional practice of human resource management. SHRM has more than 575 affiliated chapters within the United States and subsidiary offices in China, India and United Arab Emirates. Visit us at shrm.org.

Interior and Cover Design: Auburn Associates, Inc.

Library of Congress Cataloging-in-Publication Data

Danaher, Maria Greco.
   Give your company a fighting chance: an HR guide to understanding and preventing workplace violence / Maria Greco Danaher.
      pages   cm
   Includes bibliographical references and index.
   ISBN 978-1-58644-365-8
   1. Violence in the workplace. 2. Personnel management. I. Title.
   HF5549.5.E43D35 2014
   658.4'73—dc23
                         2014016024

Ogletree Deakins/SHRM
Employment Law Series
Series Editor: Jathan Janove

Contents

Introduction

Which of these recent situations can be classified as a "workplace violence" incident?

1. The 2011 shooting of Congresswoman Gabrielle Giffords at a shopping center in Phoenix, Arizona, in which six people were killed, including a six-year-old child and a local state court judge.
2. The Sandy Hook Elementary School shootings in December 2012, in which 20 children and 6 adults were killed and a trap was set for law enforcement officials investigating the incident.
3. The kidnapping of a five-year-old student from a school bus in Alabama in February 2013.
4. The one-punch fistfight between two employees in a public parking garage during a workday, over an ongoing dispute involving a client.
5. A tire-slashing incident in an employee parking lot, after a romantic break-up between a supervisor and her subordinate.

The answer, of course, is "all of the above." In each of these circumstances, the event involved either a "workplace" (town hall meeting of a governmental official, a movie theater, an elementary school, a public school bus) or an employee (fight participants, supervisor, and subordinate).

Every day, employers—typically through their human resource departments—are faced with the daunting task of trying to anticipate and prevent workplace violence, for both legal and basic human safety reasons. What can employers do to prevent violence in the workplace? How do you spot the potential perpetrators—the jilted spouse, the angry fired employee, the sullen third-shift worker, the quiet drug abuser—all of whom can be found in most workplaces? Once a potential problem has been recognized, what should be done?

Addressing workplace violence is a challenging task, and one that frequently includes skills that are not typically included in the training received by HR managers and staff. In addition to the basic moral and human desire to keep workers safe from harm, increasing legal responsibilities (including directives from the Occupational Safety and Health Administration) make violence prevention and intervention a top priority for employers, which increasingly rely on HR professionals to handle the issues. Yet handling these challenges fairly, legally, and comprehensively is not easy and involves more than a little understanding of the psychological issues at the basis of any potentially violent action.

This book is meant to provide assistance by outlining some parameters for understanding and preventing violence, for preparing for violent situations that may develop in your workplace, and for planning a response to any such incident if it does occur. Although there is no way to violence-proof any place of employment, there are means to minimize the possibility that your workplace will be the target of a violent incident.

I

Preventing Workplace Violence

1

Understanding the Statistics

Originally, and until fairly recently, the term "workplace violence" was limited to aggressive physical acts by an employee or ex-employee against a co-worker or supervisor. That term has expanded substantially to include not only acts by individuals other than employees or former employees but actions or communications meant to cause mental or emotional harm. Currently, workplace violence is viewed—by employers, employees, courts, and legislators—as any act of aggression, physical assault, or threatening behavior that occurs in a work setting and causes physical or emotional harm to customers, co-workers, or managers.

To deal with the issues of violence and potential violence in the workplace, employers must understand the recent statistics related to that violence. In March 2011, the U.S. Department of Justice (DOJ) released information related to workplace violence for the period of 1993 through 2009 (the most recent year for which data were available at the time of the survey), with emphasis on the more recent period of 2002 through 2009.

In that survey, the DOJ defined workplace violence as "nonfatal violence (rape/sexual assault, robbery, and aggravated and simple assault) against employed persons age 16 or older that occurred while they were at work or on duty." The DOJ specifically did not include workplace homicides (employees who were "killed while at work or on duty") or death-by-accident in its statistics. The DOJ defines non-workplace violence as "nonfatal violence (rape/sexual assault, robbery, and aggravated and simple assault) against employed persons age 16 or older that occurred while they were not at work or on duty."[1]

A number of the various statistical findings in the DOJ's report indicate trends that may be of interest to companies and their HR managers.

Test Your Knowledge

1. From 2002 to 2009, the rate of nonfatal workplace violence declined by:
   a. 50 percent
   b. 35 percent
   c. 5 percent

Between 2002 and 2009, the rate of nonfatal workplace violence declined by 35 percent. Interestingly, workplace violence declined more rapidly for females than for males during that period (43 percent decline for violence against women, and 29 percent against males).

2. The decline in the average annual rate of workplace violence between 2002 and 2009 was ____ the decline in the rate of nonworkplace violence:
   a. higher than
   b. lower than
   c. nearly equal to

The 2009 rate of workplace violence was 35 percent lower than the 2002 rate of workplace violence, and the 2009 rate of nonworkplace violence declined by 37 percent during that same period, a nearly equal decline. However, according to the DOJ, the average annual rate of workplace violence during that period was about one-third the rate of nonworkplace violence (5 violent crimes per 1,000 persons for workplaces versus 16 violent crimes per 1,000 persons for nonworkplaces).

3. Between 2005 and 2009, the greatest proportion of nonfatal workplace violence was committed by:
   a. supervisors
   b. strangers
   c. jilted lovers

During that period, strangers committed about 53 percent of workplace violence that was committed against males, and 41 percent of the workplace violence that was committed against women. Between one-quarter and one-third of violent incidents were committed by individuals with whom the victim had an actual work relationship (customer/client/patient/co-worker).

4. Between 2005 and 2009, firearms were used in 5 percent of nonfatal workplace violence, but shootings accounted for __ percent of workplace homicides:

    a. 0

    b. 80

    c. 14

Firearms were involved in 80 percent of workplace homicides during that period. However, according to the DOJ statistics, weapons were less likely to have been present in workplace violence than in nonworkplace violence (18 percent in workplace violence, as opposed to 27 percent in nonworkplace incidents), and firearms were present in 5 percent of workplace violence, as opposed to 10 percent in nonworkplace violence.

5. Between 2005 and 2009, the highest rate of workplace homicide victims was in the profession of:

    a. education

    b. law enforcement/protective services

    c. sales and office

In nearly one-third of workplace homicides between 2005 and 2009, the victim worked in a sales-related or office job (32.8 percent). Law enforcement/protective services made up 17.2 percent of the number, with education/training/library services at 0.6 percent.

6. The rate of workplace violence was greater than the rate of nonworkplace violence among:

    a. law enforcement officers

    b. workers in technical/industrial schools

    c. custodial care occupations

    d. all of the above

According to the DOJ, the rate of workplace violence was greater than the rate of nonworkplace violence for several occupations examined, including all of the above. Though both law enforcement officers and security guards were among the occupations with the highest rates of workplace violence, they did *not* have the highest rates of nonworkplace violence among the groups reviewed for the survey. This raises the interesting—and relevant—question of whether the self-defense or perception/awareness training provided to these individuals within their work responsibilities may provide a level of protection to them when they are not engaged in their profession.

⚖️ ⚖️ ⚖️

How can knowledgeable HR professionals use this information? First, the statistics seem to indicate that employers are doing something correctly, given that according to the DOJ survey, the rate of workplace violence continually decreased over the period reviewed. Second, from a few of the factoids above, we may be able to deduce that individuals within occupations that require them to "be prepared" for violent incidents (law enforcement and security personnel) seem to have an unexpectedly low rate of fatalities. How can we put those facts to work in preventing workplace violence? As a first step, employers and their HR departments should be or become knowledgeable about available resources, and about the legal rights and obligations associated with those resources.

2 | The Use of Pre-Employment Screenings

In recent years, and as part of ongoing efforts to decrease incidents of workplace violence, employers have frequently turned to background checks[1] and pre-employment screenings in an attempt to be proactive with respect to hiring and to ensure that employees are not exposed unnecessarily to potentially violent individuals. Third-party background verification firms are often used to provide information regarding criminal background, court records, driver's license verification, and basic identity information.

An employer that relies on a third-party background check provider should make sure to relay the employer's concern and requirement—preferably in writing—that the background checks done on behalf of the company comply with all federal, state, and local laws and regulations. Such a written confirmation can be used as evidence of the employer's good faith intention to comply with the applicable laws.

Using the Internet to Search for Background Information

Although some employers view the Internet as an economical and fast way to conduct background checks on applicants and potential employees, such use should only be undertaken after review of the legal limitations of that tool.

Employers should be aware of ways in which an Internet search of an individual's background can create legal ramifications. For instance, viewing an applicant's Facebook page or Twitter postings could include viewing photos that reveal an individual's age, race, or disability. If the applicant is not hired, an argument could be made by that person that the basis of the unsuccessful application was a protected characteristic, which could lead to unintended legal liability for the employer.

Therefore, employers that make a decision to use the Internet for any part of a background check should make that decision with a conscious regard for the risks associated with doing so.

EEOC Guidance on Background Checks

Most employers are familiar with the requirements of the Fair Credit Reporting Act (FCRA),[2] which spells out the permissible uses of consumer reports, including criminal background histories, and outlines compliance procedures. The act is administered by the Federal Trade Commission (FTC).

However, fewer employers are aware of the fact that in April 2012, the Equal Employment Opportunity Commission (EEOC) consolidated and updated its prior guidance documents regarding the use of criminal histories in employment decisions in its *EEOC Enforcement Guidance: Consideration of Arrest and Convictions Records in Employment Decision under Title VII of the Civil Rights Act of 1964.*[3]

That guidance is a compilation of the EEOC's past policy documents and prior court decisions regarding the commission's position that employers' reliance on arrest and conviction records may have a negative impact on individuals because of race or national origin.

In that guidance, the EEOC focused on "disparate impact" discrimination, which occurs when an employer's neutral background check policy or practice disproportionately affects individuals in a protected category. This may occur when an employer refuses to hire individuals with any evidence of a prior arrest record in their background, whether recent or past, based on an unsupported fear that such an individual may be more likely to engage in workplace violence.

Employers should be prepared for increased requests from the EEOC for applicant and hiring data on this issue. However, an employer that is charged by the EEOC with discrimination related to background checks may counter with an "affirmative defense" to such an allegation, by providing evidence and documentation that the company's background check policy or practice is job-related and consistent with business necessity.

In the guidance, the EEOC identifies two circumstances in which an employer can establish the "job-related and consistent with business necessity" defense. The first requires a formal validation study or a detailed analysis of criminal conduct as related to subsequent work performance or behaviors, an esoteric standard that most private employers are not readily able to meet.

The second, however, is more accessible, although more time-consuming and effort-intensive. It involves the development by the employer of a "targeted screening process" for all applicants, setting parameters for the nature and gravity of offenses or conduct that will exclude an applicant; the amount of time that has passed since the offense, conduct, or completion of the sentence; and the nature of the job held or sought.

Once a group of applicants has been screened using these factors, each of those applicants should then be allowed an individualized review of his or her specific criminal background issue. The guidance essentially establishes a *de facto* requirement for individualized screening of applicants and candidates by stressing that an employment screening process that does not include individualized assessments is "more likely" to violate Title VII of the Civil Rights Act.

Importantly, the EEOC reiterates in the guidance a position that it has put forth in numerous past cases: that an arrest, without more, can *never* be "job-related and consistent with business necessity" because an arrest does not establish that criminal conduct has occurred. Under the U.S. criminal justice system, individuals are presumed innocent until proven guilty, and an arrest does not necessarily lead to a conviction establishing guilt.

Therefore, employers should not make hiring decisions based on arrest records, without more—including, at least, some documentation of an ultimate conviction on the arrest—even if there is a fear or suspicion that the applicant's behavior may be a precursor to workplace violence.

The most troublesome aspect of the EEOC guidance, and one that is likely to be the subject of discussion and, possibly, legislation in the future, is the EEOC's specific statement that employers should work to "eliminate policies or practices that exclude people from employment based on any criminal record."

This one-line directive is certain to raise some concern among employers, especially in conjunction with recent developments in "ban the box" legislation in various states and municipalities, which preclude employers from asking for prior criminal convictions until after an initial interview (and thereby banning the box on an application to "check here if you have been convicted of a crime in the past"). Most of the laws passed to date simply require that the "box" be removed from an initial application—which means that everyone gets a chance at a first interview, regardless of criminal background issues.

The challenge for HR professionals under these circumstances is to verify that any ultimate exclusion of applicants on the basis of criminal background is clearly "job-related and consistent with business necessity" to avoid negative attention from the EEOC, while at the same time ensuring the general safety of its employees.

The OFCCP's New Regulations

In addition to the EEOC and the FTC, the U.S. Department of Labor's Office of Federal Contract Compliance Programs (OFCCP) has also thrown its hat into the pre-employment screenings ring by issuing regulations that call for increased obligations and affirmative action regarding the hiring of individuals with disabilities by companies that are government contractors.[4]

The regulations expand the scope of recruitment and hiring of individuals with disabilities, as well as data collection and reporting requirements for contractors subject to OFCCP review. The overlap between the pre-employment screening regulations and workplace violence comes in the area of mental impairment or psychological disabilities.

Employers that overestimate the impairment associated with an individual's psychological or mental disability, or react out of misplaced fear that such impairment will always directly lead to a violent incident, may find themselves under the scrutiny of the OFCCP, pursuant to these regulations.

One of the regulations' most critical provisions, however, is one requiring contractors to provide training to personnel involved in recruitment, hiring, promotion, and disciplining. That training should include the contractor's affirmative obligations under the regulations and should outline the benefits of employing individuals with disabilities, as well as inform such personnel of the contractor's legal obligations in this area.

Comprehensive, objective training in this area can help alleviate some of the burden that the new regulations are perceived to impose. It could also help broaden the understanding often associated with mental or psychological impairments.

OPM and the EEOC on Integrity Testing

In addition to background checks, some employers have instituted "integrity testing" in an attempt to screen out individuals who may be prone to violence or dishonesty. According to the U.S. Office of Personnel Management (OPM), "integrity testing" is a "specific type of personality test designed to assess an applicant's tendency to be honest, trustworthy, and dependable."[5] Employers often associate a lack of integrity with counterproductive workplace behaviors, including theft and workplace violence.

Problems can arise when an integrity test includes questions that may require an applicant to reveal personal information regarding his or her protected class or regarding an actual or perceived medical psychological impairment. In those instances, the test could be violating federal antidiscrimination laws.

In September 2013, the EEOC was asked by an entity that "conducts integrity testing of employment applicants for third parties" to comment on specific questions included in an integrity test. The test at issue asked applicants: (1) to describe current use of methamphetamine; (2) to set forth any current use of illegal, non-prescription drugs at work; and (3) whether they would "take things from their employer without permission to get even if they felt that the employer (either the company or their boss) was treating them unfairly." The EEOC issued an "informal discussion letter" in response to the inquiry.[6]

Upon review, the EEOC first opined that because the test questions "do not ask applicants to disclose their arrest or conviction history," they do not implicate Title VII liability related to discriminatory use of criminal history information. Title VII does not prohibit employers from asking applicants about current illegal drug use or the illegal use of non-prescription drugs at work, nor does it preclude an employer from asking an applicant hypothetical questions about how the applicant might react in situations that may involve illegal activity. However, the EEOC was careful to point out that an employer still may violate Title VII if evidence indicates that an integrity test was "designed, intended, or used" to discriminate against certain applicants because of protected characteristics. Further, such a test can violate Title VII if the results are adjusted or altered to screen out certain applicants in protected categories.

The EEOC then indicated that the subject integrity test also would not violate the Americans with Disabilities Act (ADA). While pre-employment tests cannot ask disability-related questions or questions that are likely to elicit information about a disability, the ADA does not protect individuals who currently are using illegal drugs and, therefore, an inquiry on that issue does not violate the statute. However, question related to past drug addiction, use, or treatment, would, in fact, be viewed by the EEOC as violating the ADA's prohibition on disability-related questions.

While an informal discussion letter from the EEOC does not constitute an official opinion, it indicates the position of the EEOC on a specific set of circumstances. Because the letter also sets forth certain circumstances in which the EEOC would have decided differently, it is an important roadmap for employers who are inclined to use integrity testing in their application process as a tool for avoiding workplace violence.

3

Employers' Legal Duty to Keep Employees Safe

It is a continuing challenge to HR professionals to adhere to federal, state, and local laws while at the same time working to ensure the health and safety of employees.

As most employers are aware, employee safety is a specific requirement of the General Duty Clause of the Occupational Safety and Health Act (OSH Act). Under that clause, employers are required to provide their employees with a place of employment that is "free from recognizable hazards that are causing or likely to cause death or serious harm to employees."[1]

The courts have interpreted the General Duty Clause to mean that an employer has a legal obligation to provide a workplace free of recognized hazardous conditions or activities that cause, or are likely to cause, death or serious physical harm to employees when there is a reasonable method to abate the hazard. The Occupational Safety and Health Administration (OSHA) has the power to enforce deviations from that duty and to impose fines and penalties for violations.

Under the General Duty Clause, an employer that has experienced acts of workplace violence, or becomes aware of threats, intimidation, or other indicators showing that the potential for violence exists within the workplace, would be on notice of the risk of workplace violence and should implement a workplace violence prevention program combined with engineering controls, administrative controls, and training.

One clear example of the OSHA's views related to the reporting of workplace violence is illustrated in a 2009 interpretation letter issued by OSHA's Directorate of Evaluation and Analysis.[2]

The letter was a response to an employer's questions as to whether a specific incident of violence was work-related and therefore reportable. The incident involved two supervisors who had completed their work for the day and had entered a trailer to change clothes before going home. Their bantering escalated into a physical confrontation where one supervisor allegedly pulled a knife, striking the other and causing a laceration that required sutures to close.

OSHA responded first by stating that "[v]iolence in the workplace does not generally qualify as an exception" to the recordkeeping rule imposed upon employers. It went on to expressly state, however, that recording an incident does not indicate that an employer or employee was at fault or that an OSHA standard was violated.

Importantly, the letter stated that injuries and illnesses reported by an employer do not necessarily indicate an employer's lack of interest in safety and health:

> Recording a case indicates only three things: (1) that an injury or illness has occurred; (2) that the employer has determined that the case is work-related (using OSHA's definition of that term); and (3) that the case is non-minor, i.e., that it meets one or more of the OSHA injury and illness recording criteria—in this case, the fact that stitches were required to close the wound.

It can be assumed from this letter that OSHA will take a broad view when determining whether an incident involves "workplace violence." That, coupled with the General Duty Clause's requirement that employers who do not take reasonable steps to prevent or abate a recognized hazard in the workplace create risk for employers who fail to develop and enforce a workplace violence policy.

OSHA's Workplace Violence Enforcement Directive

OSHA's position regarding workplace violence was formalized when the agency issued a written enforcement directive to assist its employees in investigating and dealing with incidents of workplace violence.[3]

The directive, issued in September 2011, is to be used by OSHA's district supervisors and area directors in determining whether to conduct an investigation into allegations of workplace violence, and includes inspection procedures that will be followed by the agency's compliance officers while conducting such inspections. It also suggests various acceptable methods of abatement available to employers in workplace violence situations.

The directive expands the typical definition of workplace violence to include "threats of assault," as well as actual assaults directed toward individuals at work or on duty. Though OSHA advises that inspections by its investigators "generally shall not be considered" if the allegation of workplace violence is based solely on threats by co-workers, the directive further states that OSHA may refer such incidents to the appropriate criminal enforcement agency, or to the Equal Employment Opportunity Commission (EEOC) or the National Labor Relations Board (NLRB), for follow-up investigation if the report is deemed to include "instances that could be classified as intimidation or bullying."

The directive also spells out various risk factors that may indicate the potential for workplace violence. These include:

- Working with unstable/volatile persons in certain health care, social service, or criminal justice settings.
- Working alone or in small groups.
- Working late at night or during early morning hours.
- Working in high-crime areas.
- Guarding valuable property or possessions.
- Working in community-based health or drug abuse clinics.
- Exchanging money in certain financial institutions.
- Delivering passengers, goods, or services.
- Working in mobile workplaces (for example, taxi drivers).

OSHA inspections may be initiated following a complaint, referral, fatality, or catastrophic event (which is defined in the directive as hospitalization of three or more employees) involving an incident of workplace violence, and are more likely in high-risk industries or workplace settings that include the cited risk factors. Employers may face citations for potential workplace violence issues during programmed inspections.

The directive lists certain specific actions or mechanisms available to employers to minimize or eliminate the risk of workplace violence (including alarm systems, panic buttons, and hand-held alarms). According to OSHA, administrative controls could also include establishing liaisons with local police and state prosecutors, implementing a mandatory reporting policy, maintaining a log book of all reported assaults or threats, and advising employers of procedures for requesting police assistance or filing charges.

The further extension of OSHA into incidents and threats of violence is an event to which employers should pay close attention. The extent and manner in which workplace violence is managed by an employer will directly affect its ability to defend against OSHA citations and other potential civil or criminal proceedings related to such incidents.

Prohibiting Weapons in the Workplace

Currently, there is no federal law that regulates weapons at private workplaces—the enforceability of an employer's prohibition on weapons in the workplace, therefore, rests primarily on state laws.[4] However, beginning with Oklahoma, several states have passed laws related to guns in the workplace. These laws—sometimes referred to as "parking lot laws"—vary widely in terms of their restrictions (see textbox below).

In addition, at this time, most state laws are written and implemented to regulate members of the general public, and not "employees"; therefore, an employer cannot always rely on the OSH Act's requirements for workplace safety to preclude weapons possession by employees.

In 2012, the Supreme Court of Kentucky reversed a holding in which a lower court supported the firing of an anesthesia technician at the University of Kentucky's Chandler Medical Center.[5] The technician

Weapons at Work

More than a dozen states have passed varying laws recognizing an individual's right to store an otherwise lawfully possessed firearm in a locked personal vehicle when it is parked on the employer's property.

For example, under Louisiana law, an employee who lawfully possesses a firearm may transport or store the firearm in a locked, privately owned motor vehicle in the employer's parking lot, parking garage or other designated parking area. However, the law also allows employers to require that the firearm be hidden from plain view or locked in a case within the vehicle. *La. Rev. Stat. Ann. § 32:292.1 (2011)*.

Mississippi employers with parking areas to which general public access is restricted or limited through a security measure (for example, a gate or clearance area) can prohibit employees from transporting or storing firearms in their vehicles. *Miss. Code Ann. § 45-9-55(2) (2011)*.

While North Dakota's parking lot law establishes an employee's right to have a gun in a personal vehicle, if that vehicle is locked, the law does not apply to any motor vehicle that is owned, leased or rented by the employer or the landlord of the employer. *N.D. Cent. Code § 62.1-02-13(6)(e) (2011)*.

Because of these varying laws, it is difficult to generalize about specific situations— for instance, whether an employer can preclude an employee from parking his or her car in the company's parking lot if the employee carries a firearm in the car at all times.

was fired for having a loaded semiautomatic weapon in his car in the university's parking lot in violation of the university's policies.

In reversing the lower court's decision, however, the state's supreme court found that the medical center had violated public policy when it fired the technician for exercising a right allowed to him under the state law.

Here are the facts of the case: After a report by a hospital coworker, an anesthesia technician was asked whether he was keeping a firearm in his locker, which was prohibited by the university's rules. He denied that fact, but admitted to having a semiautomatic pistol in his car, which was parked on university property.

The pistol was confiscated by the officers pursuant to the university's policy against possession of a deadly weapon on university property or while conducting university business, and the individual's employment was then terminated under the same policy. The employee filed a lawsuit, and the lower court upheld the firing.

In response to the appeal by the technician, the university pointed to a Kentucky state law that precluded limitation on "the right of a college, university, or any postsecondary education facility . . . to control the possession of deadly weapons on any property owned or controlled by them . . . ."[6] In other words, a university typically would be allowed to limit the possession of firearms on campus.

However, the state's supreme court determined that this right is qualified by the state's "concealed deadly weapon" statute, which allows any person licensed to carry a concealed deadly weapon (as was the technician) to store such weapon and ammunition "in his or her vehicle."

Therefore, that Kentucky statute forbids public and private organizations—including universities and hospitals—from prohibiting deadly weapons anywhere in a vehicle, if the weapon owner is licensed to carry a concealed weapon. In this case, the fact that the weapon was in the employee's car and was not found in the actual workplace was the fact on which the case ultimately turned.

Although this case was decided under Kentucky state law and arguably applies only to situations in that state, it makes an important point: To develop, disseminate, and implement rules about weapons in the workplace, employers must have an understanding of the specific state laws related to weapons, concealed weapons, and public policy issues that might preclude enforcement of those rules.

Multistate employers that plan to develop policies related to weapons should ensure that the policy is enforceable in the various states in which the company does business.

Weapons Policy for Workplaces

The elements of a specific policy banning weapons in the workplace must be crafted with an eye toward the relevant state statutes. However, a weapons policy should include, at a minimum:

- A basic statement regarding the purpose of the policy ("To ensure a safe workplace, free of violence for all employees, [Company Name] prohibits the possession of deadly weapons on company property").
- The discipline to which a violator will be subject ("Employees in violation of this policy will be subject to immediate disciplinary action, up to and including termination").
- Definitions of relevant terms (for example, "deadly weapon"[7] and "company property").
- The limit of the company's right to search for weapons ("[Company Name] reserves the right to search company-owned vehicles, lockers, desks, and containers at its discretion for weapons; it further reserves the right to search packages, briefcases, and persons upon reasonable suspicion that a weapon is on the premises in violation of this policy").
- A statement of who will enforce the policy, and to whom reports of suspicions related to weapons should be made ("This policy shall be enforced by the [Company Name] human resource manager. All questions, concerns, and reports should be made directly to the human resource department.").

As always, it is prudent to discuss with your legal department or counsel any plan to conduct a search for weapons when that search may include arguably private areas (for example, desks, lockers) or to take any adverse employment action (discipline, demotion, or termination) against an employee for possession of a weapon, to ensure compliance with all applicable state laws and regulations.

Employee Terminations as a Catalyst for Violence

Catalysts that trigger incidents of workplace violence vary greatly and do not always involve the actions of an employee or employer. However, most experienced HR professionals have seen first-hand a violent reaction of an individual employee who has just been reprimanded, disciplined, or terminated.

To ensure that a termination meeting is as trouble-free as possible and, therefore, less likely to lead to a violent outburst or confrontation,

HR professionals should conduct meetings consistently and, if possible, according to a "script" to make sure that all points are effectively covered. This does two things: It increases the HR practitioner's comfort level because everything is written down in a checklist-type format; secondly, it increases the comfort level of the employee because the meeting will (hopefully) be smooth, unintimidating, and unemotional. To conduct a trouble-free—and therefore, incident-free—termination, direct the meeting in the following sequence:

1. Tell the employee the purpose of the meeting, communicating the reason for the termination in the most concise way possible.
2. Advise that the decision is final and cannot be reversed.
3. Tell the employee the effective date of the termination.
4. Review a written summary of continued benefits, if applicable.
5. Have the final paycheck ready, or inform the employee of when and how it will be delivered, keeping in mind any applicable state laws on time limitations for that delivery.
6. Outline any remaining steps in the process (for example, return of company equipment, remaining days of work, transition of project).
7. Tell the employee how and when notification of COBRA will be made.
8. Answer questions briefly, and without argument.
9. Wish the employee good luck.
10. Stand, extend your hand, and remain standing until the employee has left the room. (Depending on the circumstance, this step may include escorting the employee to his/her workspace to retrieve personal items and then walking him/her out of the building.)

If the termination involves an individual who has exhibited violent, disruptive, or otherwise inappropriate behavior in the past, security (or, in extreme situations, local law enforcement) should be placed on standby to avoid a time lapse between any possible violent reaction from the employee and assistance in containing that violence.

4 | Workplace Bullying

Workplace bullying is repeated perceived mistreatment of a "target" individual by another and often includes emotional abuse or other forms of psychological violence.

According to Gary Namie, the co-founder of the Workplace Bullying Institute,[1] an education, research, and advocacy organization, "we must understand that bullying is different from harmless incivility, rudeness, boorishness, teasing, and other well-known forms of interpersonal torment. Bullying is a form of violence, but only rarely involves fighting, battery, or homicide. It is mostly sub-lethal, non-physical violence."[2]

According to Namie's website, a bully's or perpetrator's behavior most often takes one or more of the following forms:

- Verbal abuse (which could include derogatory speech, dismissive or condescending remarks, taunting, or angry or inappropriate speech).
- Offensive conduct (threatening or intimidating movements or actions; posting humiliating or negative script, photos, or

drawings; or simple refusal to include an individual in a work-related social event).

- Work interference (refusal to cooperate, taking action to keep an individual's work from completion, or active sabotage).

Research has shown that workplace bullying can have serious consequences, including decreased employee morale and loyalty, reduced productivity, lack of trust among co-workers, and higher health care and workers' compensation claims.

Bullying has been compared to the phenomenon of domestic violence. Both were shrouded in silence and secrecy prior to current public efforts at attention to the issues. Domestic violence victims were often blamed for their own fate. However, as the phenomenon of domestic violence has received attention and corrective efforts, society has labeled it as unacceptable and has begun codifying laws against such action.

Workplace bullying—finally recognized through articles, court decisions, and legislative efforts—deserves the same reaction, and movement toward prohibition. The challenge for employers in this effort is that in the workplace bullying arena, the bully most often is on the same payroll as the victim.[3]

The attention generated by workplace bullying is based both on its primary effects, which include physical and emotional ailments, and on the fact that such action, without a response by the employer, has the very real potential to escalate into physical violence.

"Degrees" of Workplace Bullying

According to Teresa A. Daniel, in her book *Stop Bullying at Work*:

> A consensus seems to have developed that these various forms of hostile behaviors arrange themselves along a continuum of increasing severity. For example, behaviors captured under the terms "emotional abuse," "psychological aggression," and "incivility" are often characterized as low-intensity or low-level bullying, while forms of physical violence (such as assault, rape, and homicide) are considered to be "extreme forms" of bullying.[4]

Daniel also stated that workplace bullying has been described as an escalating process, classified by three "degrees,"[5] as follows:

- First-degree bullying: The individual manages to resist, escapes at an early stage, or is fully rehabilitated in the same workplace or somewhere else;
- Second-degree bullying: The individual cannot resist, nor escape immediately, and suffers temporary or prolonged mental and/or physical disability, and has difficulty re-entering the workforce; and
- Third-degree bullying: The physical and mental injuries are so severe that rehabilitation seems unlikely.

The Broad-Based Effects of Bullying

Though substantial information is available on the physical and emotional effects of bullying on its targets, less is known about the effects on other employees who witness the bullying and are unwilling or unable to stop it.

In a 2013 Swedish study dealing with major industries in that country—a paper mill, a steel factory, and a truck manufacturer—researchers from that government's Institute of Environmental Medicine followed workplace bullying witnesses for a period of 18 months.[6]

The study results indicate that exposure to bullying, although a vicarious experience for witnesses, is a significant risk factor in developing depression. This may be because bystanders are unable to control the situation, leading to feelings of helplessness, which could be exacerbated when they either cannot or will not come to the target's rescue.

One unusual finding was that although the number of men who were bystanders to bullying was larger compared to the number of women, female witnesses showed a higher prevalence of clinical depression (33.3 percent) than did male witnesses (16.4 percent).

Ultimately, bullying in the workplace should be prevented based on the fact that bullying is a common precursor to workplace violence. In addition, the effects of bullying—and, it seems, on bystanders to bullying—are measurable, in terms of both health and general productivity.

Cyberbullying in the Workplace

Many employers and employee groups have recognized the pervasiveness of bullying via Internet and electronic communications, which can include e-mail threats, sharing private information online, or unwanted sexual attention in the form of texts or other electronic messages.

The Australian government recently took the preemptive step of establishing a website for the express purpose of preparing young people for the responsibility of working safely and of informing them of general hazards in the workplace. Included in the list of hazards is cyberbullying.[7]

The site includes results from a survey conducted in January 2013 by Internet security company AVG Technologies involving 4,000 adults from 10 countries. One of the key findings of that survey has implications for all employers: "Half of those surveyed believed their company was responsible for the online behaviour of employees during work hours if they were using their personal social media accounts."

In addition to employees' expectations of a safe and secure workplace, employers are obligated under the Occupational Safety and Health Act's General Duty Clause and under the Occupational Safety and Health Administration's 2011 workplace violence directive[8] to provide a workplace "free from recognizable hazards," which clearly include the use of electronic communications as a mechanism for bullying.

Working to Eliminate Bullying in the Workplace

The Workplace Bullying Institute—a research, training, support, and advocacy organization encouraging individuals to participate in a grassroots movement to enact laws against workplace bullying—started in 2001, thanks to Professor David Yamada who drafted the text of the Healthy Workplace Bill (HWB). According to the group's website, the original bill grew out of Yamada's seminal legal treatise on workplace bullying and the need for "status blind harassment" laws.[9]

At the time of this writing, the HWB, which according to the institute, "plugs the gaps in current state and federal civil rights protections," has been introduced in 23 states in over 60 versions since 2003, and has been sponsored by more than 300 legislators.

Although no laws have yet been enacted, 10 states have active bills in process as of February 1, 2014.[10] Bills have passed committee votes in Connecticut, Illinois, New York, and Washington; passed house floor votes in New York for a study-only bill; and passed both houses in Illinois as a joint resolution, establishing funding for a one-year task force on workplace bullying. In 2010, the senates in both the New York and Illinois legislatures passed the bill. Clearly, the interest is there for future action.

According to the "Quick Facts" page of the Workplace Bullying Institute's website, the language of the HWB protects targets of workplace bullying by providing a basis for legal action and by allowing the victim to pursue damages for health effects, lost wages and benefits, and injunctive relief in the form of prevention and correction of future bullying instances. It also allows the target to sue the "bully" as an individual.

In addition, the bill includes language that can benefit employers by:

- Precisely defining an "abusive work environment," which includes a clearly outlined standard for recognizing misconduct.
- Requiring "proof of harm" by a licensed health or mental health professional to support a claim for damages.
- Requiring plaintiffs to use private attorneys.
- Allowing employers to terminate or sanction offenders without attendant legal liability.
- Protecting conscientious employers from vicarious liability risk when internal correction and prevention mechanisms are in place.

Of interest are the facts that the HWB does not use the term "workplace bullying" and that it is "status blind" in that it does not require a plaintiff to be a member of a legally protected minority before filing a claim under this proposed law.

The Abuse of Rank as a Symptom of Workplace Violence

One of the most interesting statistics included on the Workplace Bullying Institute's website is the fact that 72 percent of bullies "outrank" their target and that only 18 percent of bullying is engaged in by peers.

This fact has been recognized and written about at length by Dr. Robert W. Fuller:

> *Rankism* is the exploitation or humiliation of those with less power or lower status. Rankism occurs when *somebodies* use their power to take advantage of those they see as *nobodies*. As the cause of indignity, rankism is no more defensible than the familiar indignities of racism, sexism, etc. Eliminating rankism doesn't mean eliminating rank any more than getting rid of racism means getting rid of race. Rank can be a useful tool that helps us achieve group goals. It is the abuse of rank that does the damage and calls for attention.[11]

Fuller points out that in the decades following World War II, and under pressure from women and minorities, Americans finally accepted the idea that a difference between individuals based on age or race or gender is not a valid basis for discrimination against that individual. Although such discrimination was accepted during various periods of the United States's past, that discrimination is now considered unacceptable and, in fact, illegal under federal and state law.

Fuller continues, however, that despite those "successes" with certain protected characteristics, indignities, unfairness, and oppression still continue and are actually commonplace.

Most HR professionals recognize this fact, based on the complaints and concerns that are submitted to them on a regular basis by individuals outside of a legally protected class who claim unfairness or mistreatment. Those individuals are frequently at the "bottom of the totem pole" and are unlikely to move from that position at any point in the foreseeable future.

In attempting to deal with these issues, HR personnel should recognize that objects of bullying or other mistreatment seldom "absorb" that behavior and magically transform it into good or graceful behavior in themselves. Though "turning the other cheek" is admirable, it is also infrequent in such situations.

Rather than being high-minded in these circumstances, most targets simply take their negative feelings out on someone whom they perceive to be less powerful and who cannot fight back, and the pattern continues until someone quits a job . . . or the workplace erupts in violence.

If Fuller is correct, then rank is the elephant in the room (just like gender and race were in the past), and creates a situation in which certain bad behavior will continue until recognized for what it is—bullying based on workplace inequality. The importance of this fact to employers is set forth in the studies, cited above, that link bullying to increased incidents of workplace violence.

How can employers address this issue in a productive way? Fuller suggests that companies can overcome "rankism" by making sure that "all employees see better futures ahead of them."

That may seem to be an insurmountable obstacle for some companies. However, many firms already have the beginnings of such a plan: businesses that provide tuition reimbursement for employees who are making an attempt to better themselves; companies that provide recognition to individuals for innovations or completion of a challenging project; managers who spread work-related decision making beyond a particular management level to include those of lesser "rank" and job level; and allowing opportunities for upward mobility within the company, rather than hiring only from outside.

The goal of reducing "rank abuse" will have ramifications in addition to a potential lessening of workplace bullying and violence. Engaging employees' self-interest in success will include increased productivity and, ultimately, increased profit.

Anti-Bullying Policies

Although current federal anti-discrimination law does not require employers to have a policy to specifically address workplace bullying, such policies are good business practice. They lift employee morale by promoting and supporting a culture of civility throughout the workplace. Employers that are serious about their efforts to prevent workplace violence should give strong consideration to including such language in handbooks or work policies.

A workplace bullying policy could be added to a larger anti-harassment policy or to an existing handbook, or it could be issued as part of a stand-alone workplace violence policy. As in most written workplace policies, an anti-bullying policy should be tailored to the particular business, size of the company, geographic breadth of locations, and management structure; however, certain elements are common to most anti-bullying policies.

Such policies should define bullying, including specific examples of bullying behavior to allow employees to understand the types of behavior for which discipline will be imposed. In addition, policies should set forth a clear and usable reporting procedure.

Below is a list of four critical elements of an effective policy: purpose definition, types of prohibited behavior, and specific examples. In each instance, the exemplar language in bold print is taken from a template policy posted for public access on the website of the Society for Human Resource Management (SHRM).

- **The purpose of the policy:**
  The purpose of this policy is to communicate to all employees, including supervisors, managers and executives, that [Company Name] will not *in any instance* tolerate bullying behavior. Employees found in violation of this policy will be disciplined, up to and including termination.
- **A definition of "workplace bullying" (if, in fact, that is the way to which it will be referred; some employers have begun to use the more descriptive term "abusive workplace behavior"):**
  [Company Name] defines "bullying" as repeated inappropriate behavior, either direct or indirect, whether verbal, physical, or otherwise, conducted by one or more persons against another or others, at the place of work and/or in the course of employment. Such behavior violates the company's code of ethics, which clearly states that all employees will be treated with dignity and respect.
- **An explanation of the categories of behavior prohibited:**
  Bullying may be intentional or unintentional. However, it must be noted that where an allegation of bullying is made,

the intention of the alleged bully is irrelevant, and will not be given consideration when meting out discipline. As in sexual harassment, it is the effect of the behavior on the target that is important. [Company Name] considers the following types of behavior examples of bullying:

- Verbal bullying: slandering, ridiculing, or maligning a person or his or her family; persistent name calling that is hurtful, insulting, or humiliating; using a person as butt of jokes; abusive and offensive remarks.
- Physical bullying: pushing, shoving, kicking, poking, tripping, assault or threat of physical assault, damage to a person's work area or property.
- Gesture bullying: nonverbal threatening gestures, glances that can convey threatening messages.
- Exclusion: socially or physically excluding or disregarding a person in work-related activities.

- **A list of specific unacceptable behaviors:**
  The following examples may constitute or contribute to evidence of bullying in the workplace:
  - Persistent singling out of one person.
  - Shouting, raising one's voice at an individual in public or in private.
  - Using verbal or obscene gestures.
  - Not allowing the person to speak or express himself or herself (that is, ignoring or interrupting).
  - Personal insults and use of offensive nicknames.
  - Public humiliation in any form.
  - Constant criticism on matters unrelated or minimally related to the person's job performance or description.
  - Ignoring or interrupting an individual at meetings.
  - Reprimands conducted in public.
  - Repeatedly accusing someone of errors that cannot be documented.
  - Deliberately interfering with mail and other communications.
  - Spreading rumors and gossip regarding individuals.
  - Manipulating the ability of someone to do his or her work (for example, overloading, underloading, withholding information,

- setting meaningless tasks, setting deadlines that cannot be met, giving deliberately ambiguous instructions).
  - ○ Inflicting menial tasks not in keeping with the normal responsibilities of the job.
  - ○ Taking credit for another person's ideas.
  - ○ Refusing reasonable requests for leave in the absence of work-related reasons not to grant leave.
  - ○ Deliberately excluding an individual or isolating him or her from work-related activities (for example, meetings).
  - ○ Unwanted physical contact, physical abuse, or threats of abuse to an individual or an individual's property (defacing or marking up property).

In addition, the policy should include a specific reporting procedure, referencing more than one way in which complaints and concerns can be reported (for example, through human resources, through the individual's immediate supervisor, or through a company ombudsman designated specifically for that role).

In its *OSHA Field Health and Safety Manual* for its own employees, OSHA includes a "Violence in the Workplace Policy" that is worth emulating, as well.[12]

The policy includes "Purpose," "Scope," and "Definition" sections; the latter specifically defines "intimidating behavior" and "threats." In addition, the policy includes language that sets a positive expectation for its employees:

> Employees will treat all other employees, as well as customers, with dignity and respect. Management will provide a working environment as safe as possible by having preventative measures in place and by dealing immediately with threatening or potentially violent situations. No employee will engage in threats, violent outbursts, intimidation, bullying, harassment, or other abusive or disruptive behaviors.

The policy assigns responsibilities for delegating reporting and training duties to specific managerial-level individuals. It also specifically requires its employees to be familiar with the U.S. Department of Labor (DOL) "Workplace Violence Program"[13] and policy (which lists specific responsibilities for all levels of employee, including managers/supervisors, security officers, health and safety personnel, building management, and HR), and provides an intranet cite for that information.

The Internet contains many examples of anti-bullying policy language, and most of them include the elements listed above. In light of the ever-changing laws, court opinions, and regulations related to this area, it is wise to enlist the help of legal counsel to ensure that such a policy is consistent with the applicable law before disseminating it.

Training is a crucial part of addressing workplace bullying. Experts in both law and psychology emphasize that employees should know that a policy exists and what it covers in order to fully understand the expectations associated with any anti-bullying policy.

Training options include live training sessions in a large lecture format, small group training with interactive participation, and web-based or video trainings that can be undertaken by individuals. One law firm has even has developed free smartphone apps for HR professionals for use in diversity and anti-discrimination training.[14] The apps includes information about diversity within the workplace, and its connection to state and federal anti-discrimination training requirements. More employers, firms, and public entities are sure to join that band wagon as mobile phone apps increase and become more widely used.

Mobbing

"Mobbing," a phenomenon that only recently has begun to receive attention in the U.S., is a permutation of bullying that involves more than one person engaging in bully-like behavior toward a single target.

According to cultural anthropologist Janice Harper,

> mobbing is widely understood in Europe as a form of collective aggression that profoundly impacts a targeted worker's health and productivity, but less known in the U.S. where "bullying" is a more common explanation for interpersonal workplace aggression. Viewing "bullies" as the cause of workplace conflict presumes that the aggression a target endures is due to the psychopathology of a single aggressive individual, while ignoring the devastating impact of collective aggression.[15]

To keep mobbing from developing in the workplace and leading to a potentially violent incident—either against the target, or by the target in reaction to the mob—certain actions should be taken:

- Develop a code of conduct that includes a prohibition on mob-type conduct. This could be incorporated into an existing code of conduct or made part of an anti-bullying policy.
- Require employees, including management, to sign off on the policy or code. Mob leaders frequently are middle managers and supervisors who are exercising the limited power that they have over an individual of lower rank.
- Draft (or revise) social media policies to include language addressing cyberbullying. Mobbing often takes the form of group e-mails and social media posts.
- Educate and train the workforce to recognize and report instances of mobbing. Include a nonretaliation provision in the policy to ensure that an individual who reports such actions will not become the next mobbing target.

5 | Workplace Violence Prevention Programs and Strategies

Violence prevention programs should establish goals and objectives, as well as methods to reach those ends. The goals and objectives, of course, differ based on the size, complexity, and type of work done in the particular workplace for which the policy is being developed, and should be readily adaptable to different situations within that workplace. However, every violence prevention program should include the following:

- A clear explanation of the underlying policy, with a method for reporting violence, threats of violence, or potentially violent situations.
- A nonretaliation provision to allow employees to report incidents of mistreatment without fear of reprisal.
- The specific mention that a *threat* of violence will be considered the same as and dealt with in the same manner as an *act* of violence.

- A requirement that supervisors document and report acts and threats of violence to human resources (even if the supervisor believes he or she has dealt with the issues sufficiently).
- Some method of recording reports of violence, potential violence, or threatened violence so that future risk can be assessed.
- Selection of a liaison with law enforcement to allow prompt reporting in the event that assistance is required.
- An affirmation of management's commitment to the safety and health of its employees and to their protection from violence or threatened violence.

An anti-violence policy will be most effective when disseminated to all employees and used consistently to guide employee behavior. (In other words, do not use the policy only in situations when an employee has already engaged in violent behavior or threats.) Studies suggest 90-95 percent of the population will acquiesce to expectations when expectations are clear. Therefore, a clear, objective, and complete policy is beneficial for workplace security and security.

Employers concerned about "false reports" of violence may include a provision addressing that issue. However, the policy should make clear that *not* every unfounded report of violence will lead to discipline for a false report. Here is one example of such language:

> To make deliberate false accusations of workplace violence will also be considered a violation of the company's Workplace Violence Policy. In such instances, the complainant will be subject to disciplinary action, up to and including termination, at the company's discretion. Failure, after a reasonable investigation, to prove a claim of workplace violence does not—without more—constitute proof of a false and/or malicious accusation. However, if an unfounded report is found to be maliciously made or patently/obviously false, disciplinary action may be taken, at the employer's discretion.

Anti-violence policies and programs should be reviewed periodically—especially after any significant violent event—to ensure their effectiveness and current applicability.

If it is determined that an individual should be disciplined or terminated for violation of the employer's workplace violence policy, written documentation should be reviewed before taking such action.

Although the documentation required in these circumstances is no different from documentation necessary to support any disciplinary action—clear, contemporaneous, objectively written documentation—it is especially important to coordinate with HR and legal professionals to make certain that the proposed discipline or termination is not undermined by incomplete, subjectively biased, or emotion-based (as opposed to factual-based) evidence.

The 2011 ASIS/SHRM Standard

ASIS International is a preeminent worldwide organization for security professionals that develops educational programs and materials addressing broad security interests. The Society for Human Resource Management (SHRM) is the world's largest association devoted to advancing the interests of HR professionals and is likely to be familiar to most HR managers and personnel. In 2011, the two organizations published, *Workplace Violence Prevention and Intervention*, a standard that provides "an overview of policies, processes, and protocols" that can be referenced and used by organizations to identify and prevent violence in the workplace.[1]

The standard outlines a recommended scope for nearly every organization's efforts to prevent and manage workplace violence. Importantly, it spells out in detail the components of an effective workplace violence prevention and intervention program.

The section of the standard entitled "Establishing Multidisciplinary Involvement" spells out an approach to violence prevention that reflects the fact that workplace violence implicates numerous company resources, including not just human resources and management, but legal, security, union leaders, employee health and safety personnel, and public relations specialists. Effective prevention and intervention efforts will necessarily draw on the knowledge and skill of individuals in all or most of those areas.

Planning a workplace prevention program should begin with a needs assessment in order to determine the organization's general vulnerability to violence. Such an assessment could include:

- The company's general vulnerability to violence (based on the nature of the business, its geographic location, and any history of past violent incidents).
- An evaluation of existing prevention practices (comparing them to those recommended in the ASIS/SHRM standard, for instance).
- A review of the physical security already in place and the need for additional security (location of safe areas, availability of secure parking, confirming that alarm equipment is in place and working properly).

Once the assessment is complete, a usable policy can be drafted for distribution and implementation on a companywide basis.

OSHA's View of Workplace Prevention Programs

In 2009, the Occupational Safety and Health Administration (OSHA) published *Recommendations for Workplace Violence Prevention Programs in Late-Night Retail Establishments.*[2] Though the document was written with a focus on retail establishments, it includes many useful facts, suggestions, and resources applicable to other types of employers. The first section sets forth OSHA's proposal for effective violence prevention programs, explaining in detail the four components of an effective program:

- Management commitment and worker involvement.
- Worksite analysis.
- Hazard prevention and control.
- Safety and health training.

Each of the four elements is outlined and explained in a straightforward and usable manner, and is broken down into workable segments. For instance, the "Worksite Analysis" section includes directions on how to analyze and track records of violent incidents, how to conduct screening surveys to obtain information from employees, and how to establish a team to inspect the worksite and evaluate job tasks to identify hazards.

The publication's section entitled "Minimizing Risk through Engineering Controls and Workplace Adaptations" is essential, in light of OSHA's September 2011 workplace violence directive.[3] As defined in the publication about retail establishments, "engineering controls" are meant to remove a hazard from the workplace or to create a barrier between an employee and a particular hazard. In the instance of a retail establishment, for instance, one engineering control could be the limitation of window signs that might block an outside witness or law enforcement individual from viewing what is happening within the establishment, or might keep employees from viewing a disruptive person who is about to enter the establishment. Another control could be the use of (and posting signs to announce the use of) "drop safes" to limit the availability of cash. An obvious control for most workplaces is the installation and maintenance of alarm systems, panic buttons, or private channel radios.

After its description of the components of a successful workplace violence program, OSHA provides forms and checklists, including a number of self-inspection checklists to help identify present or potential workplace violence problems, and sample incident report forms that could be adapted to nonretail establishments and businesses.

Training Programs

The success of any violence prevention program hinges primarily on management's commitment to that program and on a willingness to make certain that employees are fully informed about and trained on the program. Such commitment can help ensure that adequate financial and staffing resources will be earmarked for the effort and that the program and its associated activities will be viewed as important and supported from the top of the management chain.

Training for both managers and employees is one of the primary elements of the success of a workplace violence prevention program. Human resources is the effective link between management and line employees and is critical to the dynamic interaction between those two groups. Therefore, it is human resources that should be responsible for the planning, timing, and success of that training. Though training may differ depending on the type of business, geographic location, and size of the workforce, certain aspects of the training are essential. In every situation, individuals should be trained on:

- Hazards typically found within workplaces and in the particular workplace itself.

- Reporting requirements, including to whom complaints and concerns should be reported.
- Evaluating potentially disruptive situations and applying appropriate and necessary reactive techniques (including crowd dispersal, immediate intervention, etc.).
- Problem-solving tactics, including verbal de-escalation protocols.

Workplace Dispute Resolution

Conflict in the workplace can be a precursor to a more violent incident if not handled effectively. Discussions during dispute resolution attempts should be nonconfrontational, with a focus on issues rather than on individual attitudes or communication skills. Effective dispute resolution can lead to better understanding of the conflicting goals and agendas of the employees involved, can create mutual respect (as opposed to further disagreement and continued misunderstanding), and may even lead to increased self-awareness for the individuals involved.

Although a number of tools and methods are related to conflict management and dispute resolution, the most widely known is the Thomas-Kilmann Conflict Mode Instrument (TKI).[4] This tool identifies five styles of dealing with conflict that vary in the degree of cooperation and assertiveness. Kenneth Thomas and Ralph Kilmann, the creators of the TKI, determined that every individual has a preferred style of conflict resolution and that various styles are most useful in different situations. The theory is that by becoming aware of your own conflict management style, and being informed about the styles to which others may "default" when conflicts arise, one is better able to deal effectively with conflict, or to resolve conflicts involving others.

The five TKI styles are:

1. Competitive: This style includes individuals who tend to know what they want and take a firm stand to get it. Individuals in this category typically operate from a position of power (position/rank/expertise) and can be effective when a decision must be made in a hurry, or when a decision is unpopular. The downside of this style is that it leaves others feeling left out and resentful when it is used in less urgent decisions, and it may be ineffective in avoiding a violent situation.

2. Collaborative: These individuals try to meet everyone's needs. Though they may be assertive, collaborative individuals also tend to cooperate effectively and to acknowledge input from others. This style is useful to bring together various views or to smooth out conflicts within a decision-making group.

3. Compromising: Individuals who exhibit this style try to find a solution that will at least partially satisfy everyone, and they expect everyone to "give up" something. This style works in an impasse, when the problem could be solved if each of the parties compromises.

4. Accommodating: This style often surrenders a position even when surrender is not warranted. These individuals are willing to meet the needs of others at the expense of the ac-commodating person's own needs. This style is appropriate when the issues matter more to the other party. In actuality, this style is generally unlikely to lead to mutually beneficial outcomes.

5. Avoiding: Typified by delegation of decision-making respon-sibilities, this style seeks to evade the conflict entirely and might be appropriate when victory is impossible. However, in most situations, this approach is ineffective in dispute resolu-tion, or in avoiding violent situations.

Once the various styles are understood, they can be used to de-velop the most appropriate approach or mixture of approaches for use in any particular conflict, and to help to de-escalate confrontations be-fore violence occurs. The optimal situation is one in which a problem solver can adopt an approach that meets the situation to resolve the problem while at the same time respecting the parties' legitimate inter-ests and working to improve damaged working relationships.

De-escalation Techniques

After a working understanding of conflict management styles is ob-tained, verbal de-escalation techniques, which can help prevent or de-fuse a potentially violent situation, can be taught and practiced. One of the principles in verbal de-escalation is that an angry or potentially dangerous person cannot be "reasoned" with—an admonition to "calm down" often has the opposite effect and may simply exacerbate the situation. Instead, small, neutral movements and comments are more likely to diffuse a potentially dangerous situation. Using the following techniques may also help:

- Maintain an open stance—no hands in pockets or crossed arms.
  - You may try to de-escalate the situation by talking to the other person, but your body language may show a willingness to get physical or an unwillingness to listen.
  - Use nonintrusive gestures (such as nodding of your head, saying "okay," or asking a legitimate question).
- Speak calmly, allowing time for response, and do not interrupt.
  - Exhibit engagement and interest by using eye contact, but do not stare.
  - A controlled voice—calm, but firm—promotes confidence in both parties.
- Ignore insulting or abusive comments, but provide answers to legitimate questions to encourage discourse.
  - Try to refocus the other person on something positive.
  - Do not become defensive or engage in argument.
- Allow physical distance from the individual.
  - Invasion or encroachment into personal space may heighten the other person's anxiety.
  - Stay far enough away that the other person cannot hit, kick, or grab you.
- Avoid aggressive actions (finger pointing, raised voice, sudden movements).
  - Use slow and deliberate movements—quick actions may surprise or scare the other person.
  - Avoid becoming emotionally involved—control your emotions at all times.

The three most important points in the de-escalation process are to:

- Stay calm.
- Be patient.
- Remain respectful of the other party.

Techniques for Preventing
Violent Incidents on Company Premises

The primary safety concern articulated by employees—especially female employees—involves walking in a parking lot or to public transportation alone and after dark. Whereas the best possible technique for dealing with an actual violent confrontation is participating in a formal self-defense training class, a number of tips can be shared with employees, formally or informally, that may help lessen the prospect of such incidents on company premises:

- **Have car keys in hand when approaching your car.** It saves you from standing next to your car while rummaging through a bag or purse; also, keys can be used as a weapon in response to a physical assault.
- **Only unlock the driver's door.** Automatic door un-lockers make it too easy to "double beep" and open a passenger door, inadvertently allowing access to an intruder.
- **After getting in to the car, lock the doors.** Many of us take a minute to read e-mails, change the radio station, or make a call after getting into the car, allowing an intruder to open an unlocked door.
- **Do not leave packages or valuables in open view, whether or not you are in the car.** There is no reason to create an invitation to an intruder who may believe that your gym bag is a bank-deposit bag full of cash.
- **Carry a cellphone when walking alone to the parking lot or to public transportation.** The caveat here is *not* to be on the phone while walking, which may distract you from being aware of someone's approach but to have quick access for a 911 call, if necessary.
- **Attach a whistle to your key chain.** In the event of an emergency, noise is attention-getting and creates commotion to discourage an attacker from staying around.
- **If something about the scene makes you uncomfortable, go for help immediately.** Being aware of your surroundings is important; if something feels wrong to you, it probably is.

II

Preparing for Violent Situations in the Workplace

6 | Categories of Workplace Violence

According to a report issued by the Federal Bureau of Investigation (FBI), workplace violence can be divided into four major categories,[1] each of which includes a violent act by an individual against a company's employee(s):

- Type I: The agent has no legitimate relationship to the workplace and usually enters the workplace to commit a robbery or other criminal act. This is sometimes referred to as an "external threat" of violence. Most recent statistics report that this type represents the largest category (by number of incidents) of workplace violence.
- Type II: The agent is either the recipient or the object of a service provided by the affected workplace or the victim. This type includes current and former patients, clients, customers, passengers, criminal suspects, and prisoners.
- Type III: The agent has an employment-related involvement with the workplace. Usually this type involves an assault or other violent act by a current or former employee toward a co-worker, supervisor, or manager.

- Type IV: The agent has no direct relationship to the workplace, but typically is a current or former spouse, lover, relative, or friend of an employee.

According to the FBI report, "Type I violence by criminals otherwise unconnected to the workplace accounts for nearly 80 percent of workplace homicides. In these incidents, the motive is usually theft, and in a great many cases, the criminal is carrying a weapon, increasing the likelihood that the victim will be killed or seriously wounded." This type of violence occurs more frequently in workplaces whose line of business make employees vulnerable to such incidents. Late-night retail and service station clerks, individuals who work in isolated locations or dangerous neighborhoods, and taxi-cab drivers are the individuals with the highest risk of being killed on the job in a Type I violence situation.

Preventive strategies for Type I incidents—involving external threats of violence—include an emphasis on physical security measures and on the implementation of policies and employee training. The fact that there has been a decline in workplace homicides in the past 25 years may be attributable to security measures put in place by businesses that are vulnerable to this type of activity. In addition, in the aftermath of the events of 9/11, knowledgeable employers have become diligent about continuing to add and develop protections against external threats to their employees.

In Type I violence situations, the interpersonal aspects of violence prevention that apply to the other categories are less relevant. Therefore, even though Type I events represent a large share of workplace violence and human resources should be aware of how these types of events are resolved, company personnel are less likely to be involved in the investigations, findings, and collection of information and evidence related to the incidents. Those activities are typically undertaken by local law enforcement.

Type II violence incidents involve assaults on an employee by a customer, a patient, or someone else receiving a service provided through the employer. Although the protagonists in this type of violence technically constitute "external threats," the fact that they have some connection to the workplace itself differentiates this type of violence from Type I. In general, Type II violent acts occur as workers are performing their normal job responsibilities. Certain occupations (for example, law enforcement, security guards) inherently include dealing with dangerous or unpredictable individuals; however, for other occupations, violent reactions by a customer or client are unpredictable. Such reactions can be triggered by an argument, disappointment or frustration at the quality of service or denial of service, or some other nonviolent event.

Employees experiencing the largest number of Type II violence are those in health care occupations and include nurses, doctors, and aides, especially those who deal with psychiatric patients; emergency medical response team members; and hospital employees who deal directly with the public (admissions clerks, emergency room staff, and crisis or acute care unit personnel). Employers in those businesses and similar businesses must assess their physical workplaces to ensure security and safety measures are up-to-date, in working order, and effective.

Type III and Type IV violence, which involves violence by past or present employees (Type III) and acts committed by domestic abusers or arising from other personal relationships that follow an employee into the workplace (Type IV), are the types widely experienced among employees. The violence in Type III and Type IV scenarios comes from an employee or someone close to an employee, so there is a much greater chance that some warning sign in the form of observable behavior will have developed to the point that notification is passed along to the employer and, hopefully, to human resources. That information, coupled with the company's violence prevention program, can work to mitigate the potential for violence or prevent it altogether.

A Word about Domestic Violence

Domestic violence—when violent acts are committed by a current or former domestic partner, by a current or former spouse, or by one family member against another—affects employee health and safety, decreases overall productivity, complicates workplace security issues, and can increase employers' health care costs substantially.

In addition to the lost work days and disruption suffered by victims of domestic abuse, perpetrators also may be less productive or miss work because of incarceration or legal proceedings resulting from the violence.

The Impact of Domestic Violence on the Workplace

According to the non-profit group Employers Against Domestic Violence, the impact of domestic violence offenders on the workplace reveal that perpetrators negatively affect workplace safety, productivity, and are responsible for lost time:

- 78% use workplace resources at least once to express remorse or anger, to check up on, or threaten the victim.
- 74% have easy access to their intimate partner's workplace, with 21% reporting that they contacted her at the workplace in violation of a no-contact order.
- 48% reported difficulty concentrating at work, with 19% reporting a workplace accident or near miss.
- 42% of offenders were late for work.

Source: Employers Against Domestic Violence, http://employersagainstdomesticviolence.org/effects-on-workplace/workplace-dv-stats.

Employers may be uncertain about preventive roles in addressing domestic violence or believe that domestic violence prevention is the responsibility of the family, social service organizations, or law enforcement. However, according to the U.S. Centers for Disease Control and Prevention (CDC), intimate partner violence victims lose a total of nearly eight million days of paid work each year, the equivalent of more than 32,000 full-time jobs.[2]

Efforts by employers to prevent incidents of domestic violence, or to provide resources that include counseling, paid time off, and return-to-work assistance, can have a positive effect on overall employee morale, while concurrently having a positive effect on overall business success.

Numerous organizations provide information regarding counseling and training for employers that want to learn more about domestic violence prevention and policies. Those organizations include:

- Employers Against Domestic Violence (EADV)
  http://employersagainstdomesticviolence.org
  EADV includes on its website a "model policy" for employers to include in handbooks and manuals.
- Corporate Alliance to End Partner Violence
  www.caepv.org

- Workplaces Respond to Domestic & Sexual Violence
  www.workplacesrespond.org
- Safe@Work Coalition
  www.safeatworkcoalition.org
- Futures Without Violence
  www.futureswithoutviolence.org

The Stages of Violence

Dr. Dennis Davis is a recognized expert on workplace violence, violence prevention, and conflict resolution, and has served as Ogletree Deakins' national director of client training since 2008. An internationally recognized leader in behavioral risk management, his book *Threats Pending, Fuses Burning* is widely considered to be a clear, concise, and effective guide to preventing workplace violence.[3] Davis spent more than 10 years consulting to federal, state, and local law enforcement agencies, where he used his education in clinical psychology to teach "willful compliance" techniques. He now uses his law enforcement background and experience to assist employers in dealing with violence and potential violence in the workplace.

According to Davis, the number one problem related to workplace violence is that employers generally are uninformed and unprepared for what workplace violence looks like and have trouble recognizing how it evolves and what causes it to escalate. He believes that it is vital for organizations to understand and know the signs and to have a policy in place to address workplace violence.

In his training sessions, Davis makes it a point to explain to HR professionals the "Stages of Violence," which can assist in identifying the potential for bad behavior that could escalate into a violent confrontation. According to Davis, there are three stages of violence:

- Stage One: Early Potential.
- Stage Two: Escalated Potential.
- Stage Three: Realized Potential.

The obvious goal for effective workplace violence management is to keep a fractious situation from escalating up the chain into a higher stage of violent behavior. To allow human resources to recognize the various stages, Davis provides specific examples of each level to allow employers to recognize the escalation principle. Here are some of his examples:

Stage One (Early Potential)

This is the stage at which it is easiest to intervene and change behavior.

- Objectifying and dehumanizing others (making sexual or demeaning comments).
- Challenging authority (questioning direction).
- Regularly becoming argumentative (refusing to reach resolution of problems).
- Alienating customers and clients (disruption of business).
- Originating and spreading lies about others (unsupportable allegations).
- Swearing excessively (includes sexually explicit language).
- Verbally abusing others (whether as a superior or as a co-worker).

Stage Two (Escalated Potential)

This stage still can be controlled by clear, strongly worded, and consistently enforced company policies against such behavior.

- Arguing frequently and intensely (refusal to de-escalate).
- Blatantly disregarding organizational policies and procedures (obvious insubordination).
- Stealing from the company (includes theft from other employees).
- Vandalism (destruction of company or employee property).
- Making verbal threats ("I don't get mad; I get even.").
- Conveying unwanted sexual attention or violent intentions by letter, voice mail, or e-mail (stalking/cyberstalking).
- Holding others responsible (refusing to take responsibility).

Stage Three (Realized Potential)

This stage most often requires outside assistance or law enforcement involvement.

- Physical confrontations/altercations (there is no such thing as "just a little shove").
- Displaying weapons (including firearms).
- Committing or attempting to commit assault or other violent crimes.

An effective workplace violence strategy must include measures to detect, assess, and manage bad behavior at the earliest possible stage. Because of the subjective nature of some threats, companies must set reasonably specific standards of behavior to allow employees to understand how they are expected to act and what behavior is prohibited. Policies should make clear that no one has a right to make others feel threatened under any circumstances. Also, employees should have a clear idea of where and to whom they should report threats or perceived threats, and should *never* take action on their own to react violently against a threat of violence.

Employees have a right to expect a workplace that allows them to be safe from threats, harassment, and actual violent behavior. One major change advocated by Davis in his trainings is an increased involvement in law enforcement and earlier participation by local law enforcement in prevention and early response to threats and minor incidents.

7

The Changing Role
of Law Enforcement

In traditional police work, investigations are done *after* a crime has been committed, and an investigation is focused on who perpetrated the incident and how it was done. After September 11, 2001, the role of law enforcement shifted perceptibly to a *preventive* role in which police increased their responses as soon as threats became known. Technically, the shift began earlier, as awareness and understanding of domestic violence issues increased, and the public stopped thinking of such violence as a "private" matter.

Much of the impetus for that shift began when a workplace violence incident in Wakefield, Massachusetts, roiled that community. Here is a description of the incident, provided by the town's police chief at the time, Stephen Doherty:

> On the day after Christmas in 2000, Michael McDermott, a 42 year old software tester for Edgewater Technology in Wakefield went on an office rampage. The result of McDermott's murderous rage left four women and three men, all his coworkers, dead in less than 10 minutes.

Reportedly in a dispute over the garnishment of his wages, an IRS order to be carried out by Edgewater's human resources personnel, McDermott came out of his work area with an AK-47 assault rifle, a 12 gauge shotgun, carrying a semiautomatic pistol in his pocket and proceeded to the area of human resources. He killed two persons in the reception area, continued on and shot to death five persons in the human resources area.

The Wakefield Police Department responded to numerous 911 calls as the shooting began. The police entered the building on reports from fleeing workers that there were injured persons inside the building. The police found McDermott sitting [in] a chair adjacent to the entry lobby with the weapons at his side. In the immediate vicinity were two victims who had been shot to death.

Michael McDermott was arrested and charged with seven counts of first degree murder. He pleaded insanity at his preliminary trial proceedings. After a full jury trial almost two years later Michael McDermott was convicted of the murders and sentenced to seven consecutive life terms in prison.[1]

In the years immediately following that incident, Doherty said that he wanted to move his department from "reacting to" workplace violence to "preventing it." After retiring from the police department, Doherty went on to found a critical incident prevention company and in 2004, in conjunction with Northeastern University, conducted and published the study, *Workplace Violence: Wakefield Responds*.[2]

The study presented a number of critical findings, including surprising statistics related to the reporting of workplace violence:

- Only 15 percent of the managers and 8 percent of the employees surveyed had ever reported an incident of workplace violence to the police after the incident's occurrence.
- The most common reason for not reporting is that the incident was not "important" enough.
- However, 60 percent of individuals who reported an incident were pleased with the police department's response.

These findings indicate a lack of information on the part of employees related to the purpose of incident reporting and a misunderstanding about the progression of workplace violence. As Dr. Dennis Davis pointed out in his book[3] and his trainings, there are stages of violence that are progressive—if an early stage goes undetected or unreported, it is likely that the next event will be an escalation of the first.

Police and Employer Cooperation

In "community policing" models being developed in some communities, employers and law enforcement work together to develop plans and protocols for anticipating violent workplace incidents, responding to threats of violence, participating in early interventions, and coordinating resources in the event of a violent incident.

The 2002 FBI report referenced in Chapter 6 includes a list of the elements necessary for implementing such an approach.[4] The list includes:

- Creating training for police officers on workplace violence issues and responses.
- Outreach and awareness efforts by law enforcement agencies directed at employers within their jurisdictions, encouraging them to work with police in preparing violence prevention plans and informing them that advice and assistance are available.
- Compiling and establishing contact with a list of other public and private agencies (such as mental health and social service agencies) that may be able to help in violence prevention planning or incident response.
- Setting meetings with local employers to provide contact information and procedures for reporting threats or incidents.
- Establishing guidelines for exchange of information between police and employers.
- Developing procedures for particular risk situations such as lay-off announcements or terminations of a dangerous employee.
- Site reviews, to provide input on safety improvements or plans for early response.

Though the FBI's protocol was established in 2002, its validity continues. Therefore, the protocol should be considered by human resources when working to develop a workplace violence plan. With the cooperation of and input from local law enforcement, teamwork will flow more smoothly in the event of a violent incident; such co-operation is also likely to decrease the number of violent conflicts, as employees will develop a level of confidence that problems will be re-solved at an early stage and will more likely report problems at the "Stage One" level.

The challenge for human resources in developing a cooperative relationship with local law enforcement may stem from management's fear that it will lose some amount of decision-making control if po-lice are drawn into workplace situations. Further, there may be some concern related to publicity associated with workplace incidents or investigations.

Such concerns should be discussed and clarified at an early stage of the development of any workplace violence team and should be ad-dressed realistically—before a violent incident exposes the weaknesses in a newly formed response team.

8 | Workplace Violence Programs for Small Businesses

More than 20 million employees—nearly one in every five non-governmental employees in the U.S.—work for companies with fewer than 20 employees, with another almost 20 million working for companies of between 20 and 100 workers.[1] Further, small businesses (between one and nine employees) make up roughly 80 percent of the country's private employers.

Small employers and their employees face no less risk of workplace violence than do larger companies. However, for many of those employers, the expense and effort required to establish a viable workplace violence prevention or reaction plan is unreachable. Most small companies do not have their own security force, legal advisors, or even an HR department. They are also unlikely to have an established relationship with law enforcement or any social service agencies that might be able to assist in the event of a violent incident in the workplace.

Crisis experts say small businesses tend to be more susceptible than large organizations to violent events because of the lack of security personnel and incident-response training. In addition, it is often more difficult for small companies to resume normal operations following an incident, based on the close relationships among workers in the small group.

Small businesses (or their advocacy groups) should consider approaching local law enforcement entities and social agencies with a request to work together to assist small companies. Here are some actions that can be taken by the manager of small businesses, or by individuals who hold the HR function in those businesses:

- Consider asking local agencies to add the topic of workplace violence to agendas for community programs in a proactive approach to inform the community of the issues.
- Band together with other small businesses to develop proposals for economic incentives like tax credits for managers who attend workplace violence training or who implement anti-violence plans.
- Work with larger employers in the community to develop workplace violence training or to invite a trainer or speaker to present to a number of community employers.
- Cooperate with local social service groups to create a website for the company to inform employees about anti-violence strategies.
- Coordinate with local emergency medical technicians (EMTs) and medical providers to schedule first aid, first responder, and medical (CPR) training for key employees.
- Publish a list of local assistance and support groups that work to prevent and eliminate violence in the community and, by extension, in local businesses.

The Financial Impact of Workplace Violence on Organizations

Liberty Mutual's annual *Workplace Safety Index*[2] identifies the leading causes of serious nonfatal workplace injuries, based on information obtained from Liberty Mutual's own workers' compensation insurance claims, along with information from the U.S. Bureau of Labor Statistics (BLS) and the National Academy of Social Insurance.

According to the 2012 edition, "assault/violent act" was listed as the tenth most frequent cause of nonfatal workplace injury in 2010 (the year measured for the 2012 report). Nonfatal attacks in the workplace accounted for $640 million in cost burden to employers in calendar year 2010, and have trended up by over 10 percent during the period between 1998 and 2010. That growth trend should be of concern to employers, especially small business owners, in an economy in which costs are being cut on almost every other level.

9 | Related Legal Issues

Along with the dollar-and-cents cost of workplace violence, the cost of legal liability should be of concern to all employers. Although there is no federal law that sets forth any rights or obligations for either employers or employees related to instances of workplace violence, many existing laws have been used as the basis for court opinions regarding situations that might otherwise have been designated as workplace violence.

The applicability of these laws underscores the importance of including legal counsel in the discussion and planning of policies, procedures, trainings, and documentation related to the prevention of workplace violence, as well as to decisions related to the treatment of employees involved in such instances.

The Americans with Disabilities Act

The Americans with Disabilities Act (ADA) allows an employer to require an employee to undergo a fitness for duty examination (FFDE) when health problems have had a substantial or injurious impact on an employee's job performance.

For instance, in 2010 the Ninth U.S. Circuit Court of Appeals reviewed a case[1] in which a police officer engaged in a "disruptive argument" with another officer, reported that he felt himself "losing control" when a young child was "taunting him" during a traffic stop, was reported to have struck his estranged wife by closing a door on her, and made a statement that "it doesn't matter how this all ends." Those incidents led the officer's department to send him for an FFDE, during which a physician determined that the officer was unfit for police duty and was permanently disabled by a mood disorder caused by a previous head injury.

Ultimately discharged from service, the officer filed a lawsuit in which he asserted that his employer violated the ADA by sending him for the examination because there was no actual "business-related reason" for doing so, as no violence had occurred. The court found that the ADA does not require an employer to wait until a perceived threat becomes real or to allow questionable behavior to result in injuries before sending an employee for an FFDE medical exam, particularly when the employee is engaged in dangerous work.

This decision is one example of a case in which a court recognized the conundrum in which many employers feel themselves caught with respect to threats and potential violence in the workplace, and interpreted an existing law in a manner consistent with the relevant safety issues.

Title VII of the Civil Rights Act

In addition to court decisions based on incidents of workplace violence, there have been recent developments in which violence victims have been provided an additional level of protection under federal laws to make sure that they are not discriminated against on the basis of their victim status. One specific example of that is a November 2012 guidance issued by the Equal Employment Opportunity Commission (EEOC).[2]

Neither Title VII of the Civil Rights Act (Title VII) nor the ADA specifically prohibits discrimination against individuals who may be victims of domestic or dating violence, sexual assault, or stalking. However, the 2012 EEOC guidance has employers scrambling to update anti-discrimination and workplace violence training to reflect the examples listed in that guidance, and to make managers aware of circumstances under which domestic violence victims might be the targets of discrimination under those federal statutes. In the guidance, the EEOC set forth numerous examples involving domestic violence and sexual assault victims that include disparate treatment, harassment, and retaliation scenarios under both Title VII and the ADA.

The examples of employment scenarios that may violate Title VII include an employer's decision to terminate an employee who was subjected to domestic violence because of fears related to the "drama battered women bring to the workplace" (disparate treatment); a supervisor who learns that an employee was recently subjected to domestic abuse and, viewing her as vulnerable, begins to make sexual advances toward her (harassment); and an employee who, subsequent to filing a complaint alleging that she was raped by a manager while on a business trip, is reassigned to less favorable projects (retaliation).

Examples of decisions involving violence victims that may violate the ADA are similarly varied and, in most cases, straightforward. They include an employer who learns that an applicant was a witness in a rape prosecution and received counseling for depression, and decides not to hire her because she may need time off for further treatment of that depression (perceived disability); a supervisor who tells an employee's co-workers about the employee's post-traumatic stress disorder resulting from incest (disclosure of confidential information); and an employee who tells her supervisor that she is going to complain about his dissemination of her medical information, and is told that if she does, she will not get a pay raise (retaliation).

However, the examples also include one scenario that may not immediately strike employers as a clear ADA violation: An employee who has no accrued sick leave and is not eligible for the Family and Medical Leave Act (FMLA) requests a scheduling change or an unpaid leave to obtain treatment for depression following a sexual assault, but is denied that leave because the company "applies leave and attendance policies the same way to all employees." Because most employers are typically reminded by both human resources and legal that employees should be treated in a consistent manner, and that individuals in protected categories should not be treated differently than nonprotected similarly situated individuals, this scenario may not seem to be an obvious example of an ADA violation. However, a reasonable accommodation is a change in the way things are usually done and can include modified work schedules, reassignment to a vacant position, or time off for medical treatment. That last phrase ("time off for medical treatment") clearly indicates that the EEOC has an expectation that employers will change their consistently applied leave and attendance policies if such change is necessary to accommodate the need for psychological treatment stemming from an incident of sexual assault or domestic violence.

Employers should, in fact, begin to add the issues raised in the EEOC's recent guidance to the training that is provides to managers and supervisors to avoid inadvertent violation of Title VII or the ADA. Fortunately, the EEOC's Q&A page that accompanied the 2012 guidance provides clear examples that can easily be incorporated in such training.

Age Discrimination in Employment Act (ADEA)

An HR manager for a large retail facility relayed to me the basic facts of a case from a number of years ago in which a group of "young" employees engaged in what she now understands was mobbing (see Chapter 4) against an older female employee. As the only member of the workgroup over the age of 35, the 50-something female employee tended to "mother" the younger employees, commenting on their clothing, their music, and their cellphone use and habits. The group resented her comments and began to make age-related remarks, refusing to include the older woman in any of their social get-togethers at lunch and after work.

The younger group members continued to make fun of the target over a period of months, at times adversely affecting her ability to do her work. When the target then saw, on a company bulletin board, a cartoon-type posting by the group that was clearly meant to demean her, she reacted strongly, making a verbal threat to the group members, for which she was fired pursuant to the company's "no tolerance" workplace violence policy.

However, the fired employee then sued for age discrimination and won, convincing a jury that her multiyear career of excellent service to the company was ended because a group of young employees refused to work with her because of her age.

Although "mobbing" was not considered directly by the jury (indeed, it does not seem to have been considered by the company in its decision to terminate the employee, either), it does seem to have been at least a factor in the decision to find that the woman had been terminated improperly.

Planning a Response to Violent Incidents in the Workplace

10 Responding to Violence in the Workplace

Violent incidents can occur at any time and without warning. Whether or not an incident has been predicted, a company's workplace violence policy and procedure should include a plan of action that can be activated promptly and effectively. Doing so can resolve the situation quickly and may avoid additional harm or injury.

An effective workplace violence plan includes procedures and responsibilities and should explicitly state who is responsible for which activities that will occur when a response to violence is necessary. This "team" should be considered the primary point for coordinating the activities necessary to bring the situation under control. Although every employer's plan to deal with a workplace violence incident is likely to differ in some respects, certain elements as outlined in *An Agency Guide to Workplace Violence Prevention and Response,* issued by the Commonwealth of Pennsylvania Office of Administration, are common to every circumstance.[1] They are presented below.

Personal Safety

An incident response/stabilization plan should contain information regarding the steps that will ensure safety for employees and any visitors or customers present at the time of the incident. General safety concepts or tips that may help defuse or minimize the threat of danger or harm should be designed so that they can be easily remembered by employees when needed, and should be incorporated into the plan. For instance:

- Employees should be advised to move into the safest possible location, which may include a "safe room," an area protected by furniture or locked doors, or simply exit the building.
- Escape routes should be practiced in the same way fire drills are practiced and should be the same in all instances so that employees are not forced to learn different routes for different emergency situations.
- A code word or phrase could be developed so that an employee who is feeling threatened can report that fact without alerting the aggressor.
- Employees should be trained not to negatively engage an attacker by arguing or interrupting him or her.
- Employees should be advised not to attempt to protect property or possessions over personal safety.

Coordination of Emergency Services

The response plan should address professional services (fire, ambulance, crisis intervention, and police) that may be needed in response to a situation and also include readily available contact numbers. Companies should also consider meeting with emergency service providers to review the response plan and to provide information about the work location, including floor plans and any relevant records (for example, records depicting locations of hazardous materials).

Communication

The response plan should address communication issues related to violent incidents. For example, the company headquarters should be notified as soon as possible when an incident of violence has taken place.

In addition to making emergency personnel aware of the situation, that central office should be charged with deciding whether to contact family members, the media, or others. (Of course, to avoid inconsistent communications that could lead to negative ramifications, including legal liability, only authorized individuals should have contact with media, and employees should be informed to refer inquiries or calls to that person.)

Impact on Work Schedules/Worksite

The plan should contain information related to the effect of a violent incident on work schedules, as changes may have to be considered to ensure safety. (Because some collective bargaining agreements include language related to schedule changes, union involvement may be important.) The plan should also include the specifics of a procedure to evacuate the worksite.

Legal Ramifications

The plan should also designate the person charged with coordinating the legal aspects of any necessary investigation of a violent incident. Duties of that individual would include preserving evidence (in circumstances other than those handled by law enforcement personnel) and coordinating with the company's legal counsel for issues related to potential termination of employment for instigators of the violent situation, or related to legal testimony necessary in circumstances in which witnesses will be interviewed or may testify in court.

11

Post-Incident Response: Getting Back to Normal

Post-incident response and evaluation are essential to an effective violence prevention program. The effects of a workplace violence incident do not end when the event ends. A post-incident plan must include a protocol for addressing the physical and psychological consequences to victims and witnesses affected by the traumatic event.

Because such occurrences can lead to long-term issues resulting in medical costs, emotional upheaval, and, in some instances, legal costs to the employee and employer, timely intervention is critical in an attempt to reduce long-term adverse impacts. Common reactions to an act of workplace violence will vary between individuals.

As in other aspects of a company's workplace violence plan, timely support to victims of an incident will be more effective if planned and practiced ahead of time. Lines of communication with social service agencies and medical providers should be preplanned and well-coordinated.

As mentioned in the previous chapter, the governor's office of the Commonwealth of Pennsylvania published *An Agency Guide to Workplace Violence Prevention and Response* that includes a detailed description of the possible physical, cognitive, emotional, and behavioral effects of an experience of workplace violence to assist employees in returning to normal after such an event.[1]

According to the guide, crisis reactions generally fall into several categories:[2]

> Stage 1: Emotional Reaction Stage
> Behaviors are typical of a "fight or flight" stress reaction and include disbelief, denial, and tearfulness. Physical symptoms may include racing of the heart, hyper-vigilance, disturbances of eating, sleeping, and concentration.
>
> Stage 2: Impact Stage
> Emotions intensify and may include rage, anger, grief, depression, guilt, and withdrawal. Physical symptoms also may intensify.
>
> Stage 3: Reconciliation Stage
> Individual has had an opportunity for self-evaluation of the incident, begins the process of reintegration, resolution, and closure.

The guide further states that[3]

> While it is difficult to predict how an incident will affect a given employee, several factors can influence the intensity of the traumatic effect of the incident of violence. These factors include:
>
> • The duration of the violent event.
> • The individual's involvement (victim or witness).
> • The amount/lack of perceived control the employee had during the incident.
> • The amount of injury or loss (whether property or well-being) the individual experienced.
> • Previous victimization issues.

Based on the broad range of reactions and possible psychological impacts, a strong follow-up program for employees will not only help them to deal with these problems but also help prepare them to confront or prevent future incidents of violence.

Several types of assistance can be incorporated into an employer's post-incident response. It may be constructive to include trauma-crisis counseling, critical-incident stress debriefing, or employee assistance program (EAP) monitoring to assist victims. Employers may also elect to establish an employee counseling service, peer counseling, or support groups.

Incident Debriefings

According to Dr. Dennis Davis, an employer's HR professional should schedule critical incident stress debriefings (CISDs) as soon as possible after the removal of a workplace threat—the most beneficial sessions are held within 72 hours of the event.[4]

Although the practice of implementing CISDs after an incident of workplace violence lost some of its popularity in the early years of this century, the understanding of the significance of these debriefings has increased dramatically in past years, especially after the trauma of 9/11 and the impact of recently returning military veterans.

In his article, Davis explained that[5]

> CISDs are not therapy sessions, but rather what he termed "psycho-educational" meetings. The intent of such meetings is to educate employees on what to expect as a result of the trauma stemming from the violent incident. According to Davis, there are three main phases of a CISD:
>
> 1. **Information.** In this phase, employees are given as much factual information as possible about the incident. This helps to decrease the number of rumors and myths that often follow traumatic incidents. Studies have shown that employees often experience increased levels of trauma when they are unsure of the specifics of a given situation and create worse (than reality) scenarios to fill in the blanks.
> 2. **Venting and validation.** During this phase of the CISD, participants are encouraged to share their fears and concerns, as well as other feelings. Expressing these emotions validates them, reducing anxiety in the organization and minimizing the need to talk about the incident

when employees return to work. This phase also provides an opportunity for the employer to discuss the measures and mechanisms in place to prevent or reduce the likelihood of a recurrence, further calming the situation.

3. **Prediction and preparation.** During this final phase of the CISD, the facilitator helps the employees understand what to expect next, including the stages of the investigation, whether employees will be interviewed or otherwise involved, etc.

Research has suggested that a CISD following a traumatic incident can reduce the negative impact on employees. Attendance at the debriefing should be voluntary, but employees should be encouraged to attend. It may be practical to have separate debriefings for management and nonmanagement. During the management debriefing, all managers should be told exactly what information is to be released to the workforce.

After the debriefing, a discussion of the company's EAP and/or available insurance coverage for counseling should be discussed. If the company does not have an EAP or its insurance carrier does not include a therapy allowance, Davis suggests that information regarding counseling centers and local social service agencies should be provided to employees.

Analyzing the Incident

After a workplace violence incident, it is imperative to review the situation on various levels, in order to control and minimize the adverse impact on employees and the workplace and to ensure that a similar incident does not reoccur. That review should be conducted in three phases:

1. **Defusing session.** This session is held immediately, or as soon as possible after a serious incident and should involve qualified counselors or other personnel to respond to employee questions, allow employees to understand the various aspects that they may be experiencing, and encourage employees to seek individual counseling or other services. The CISD described above fulfills this stage of the process.

2. **Debriefing session.** After the initial defusing session, a debriefing should occur. As opposed to a counseling-type session, this debriefing is a supportive process geared toward helping employees understand the type of effects that they may experience and continue to experience as a result of the event.

3. **Critiquing session.** Within two to three weeks after the violent incident, a critiquing session should be held to provide an opportunity for managers, supervisors, and human resources to review and discuss the incident response and to identify constructive and destructive elements of the response as it occurred to improve response in the future and to determine whether any changes are necessary in the anti-violence policy, the response program, or the coordination of efforts.

By assessing their worksites, implementing workplace violence plans, and frankly assessing the effectiveness of protocols after incidents, employers can identify methods for reducing the likelihood of future incidents occurring. A well thought-out, clearly written, and effectively implemented workplace violence prevention program and policy, combined with safety controls, administrative protocols, and consistent and regular training, can reduce the incidence of workplace violence in workplaces of all locations and sizes.

Afterword

How much of this information have you retained? You can find out by testing yourself on a few basic review questions. The answers are at the end of the quiz.

1. The Equal Employment Opportunity Commission's 2012 guidance on background checks reiterates a position put forth in numerous past cases: that an arrest, without more, can *never* be "job-related and consistent with business necessity" because . . . **why?**
2. The Occupational Safety and Health Administration's September 2011 workplace violence enforcement directive expands the definition of workplace violence to include . . . **what?**
3. Worker safety is a requirement of the Occupational Safety and Health Act's . . . **what?**
4. The enforceability of an employer's prohibition on weapons in the workplace rests primarily on . . . **what?**
5. **Give one or more examples** of the type of verbal abuse that may constitute workplace bullying.
6. **What** is workplace mobbing?
7. **List one** of the three most important points to remember during the de-escalation process.
8. Displaying a weapon is associated with **which stage** of violence? (Hint: There are three stages . . . and you get extra points if you remember the name of the stage.)
9. After September 11, 2001, the role of law enforcement shifted perceptibly from an investigative role to a _____ role in which police increased their responses as soon as threats became known. **What** type of role?
10. To create the most effective workplace violence plan, the relationship between employers and local law enforcement should be . . . **what?**

The answers:

1. Because an arrest does not establish that criminal conduct has occurred. (See Chapter 2.)
2. Threats of violence. (Chapter 3.)
3. General Duty Clause. (Chapter 3.)
4. State law. (Chapter 3.)
5. Derogatory speech, dismissive or condescending remarks, taunting, or angry or inappropriate speech. (Chapter 4.)
6. "Mobbing" is a permutation of bullying that involves more than one person engaging in bully-like behavior toward a single target. (Chapter 4.)
7. Stay calm, be patient, and remain respectful of the other party. (Chapter 5.)
8. The third stage ("Realized Potential"). (Chapter 6.)
9. Preventive. (Chapter 7.)
10. Cooperative. (Chapter 7.)

Appendix:

The Occupational Safety and Health Administration's
*Recommendations for Workplace Violence Prevention
Programs in Late-Night Retail Establishments*

www.osha.gov

The original pdf can be found at https://www.osha.gov/Publications/osha3153.pdf]

OSHA®

This publication provides a general overview of a particular standards-related topic. This publication does not alter or determine compliance responsibilities which are set forth in OSHA standards, and the Occupational Safety and Health Act of 1970. Moreover, because interpretations and enforcement policy may change over time, for additional guidance on OSHA compliance requirements, the reader should consult current administrative interpretations and decisions by the Occupational Safety and Health Review Commission and the courts.

This information will be made available to sensory impaired individuals upon request. Voice phone: (202) 693-1999; teletypewriter (TTY) number: 1-877-889-5627.

Recommendations for Workplace Violence Prevention Programs

in Late-Night Retail Establishments

Occupational Safety and Health Administration
U.S. Department of Labor

OSHA 3153-12R
2009

These recommendations are advisory in nature and informational in content. It is not a standard or regulation, and it neither creates new legal obligations nor alters existing obligations created by OSHA standards or the *Occupational Safety and Health Act*. Pursuant to the OSH Act, employers must comply with safety and health standards and regulations issued and enforced either by OSHA or by an OSHA-approved State Plan. These "state plan states" may have standards that address workplace violence. Employers are responsible for following the standards in the states where they have worksites. Appendix C provides a summary of existing State Plan standards addressing workplace violence. In addition, the Act's General Duty Clause, Section 5(a)(1), requires employers to provide their employees with a workplace free from recognized hazards likely to cause death or serious physical harm.

Acknowledgements

Many people and organizations contributed to this publication. OSHA wishes to thank the contributing researchers, educators, representatives of victims' groups, industry, and law enforcement personnel for their comments and suggestions.

Occupational Safety and
Health Administration

Contents

Introduction

Workplace violence, whether it is defined narrowly to include only violent criminal acts, or broadly to include verbal threats, has long affected retail workers. OSHA developed these recommendations to help late-night retail employers design and implement prevention programs tailored to the workplace violence hazards in their businesses. Existing data, while limited, suggests that late-night retail establishments, such as convenience stores, liquor stores, and gasoline stations, experience relatively high homicide and assault rates. This booklet is meant to provide guidance to retail employers so they may avoid such incidents whenever possible. By recognizing the hazards that lead to violent incidents and implementing appropriate prevention and control measures, employers will improve the safety of their workers. OSHA encourages employers to establish violence prevention programs and to track their progress in reducing work-related assaults. Although not every incident can be prevented, the severity of injuries sustained by workers can be reduced. Adopting practical measures, such as those outlined in this publication, can significantly reduce this serious threat to worker safety.

Extent of the Problem
According to the Bureau of Labor Statistics' (BLS) *Census of Fatal Occupational Injuries* for 2007, assaults and violent acts claimed 864 lives in 2007 and represented over 15% of the total 5,657 workplace fatalities in the United States. Homicides represented the majority of these violent acts, claiming 628 lives in 2007, or 11% of fatalities. Over 26% of those homicides (a total of 167) occurred in the retail trades, with 39 occurring at convenience stores, 32 occurring at gasoline stations and 7 occurring at liquor stores. While homicides have shown a marked overall decline since 1994 when they peaked at 1,080, they were the third leading cause of work-related deaths in 2007, and remain a serious risk for late-night retail workers.

Data from the BLS Survey of *Occupational Injuries and Illnesses* for 2007 suggests that non-fatal violent incidents have also impacted retail work sites. Overall, private industry experienced a 2.6 incidence rate[1] for assault and violent acts (a total of 24,230 incidents) but convenience stores experienced a rate of over 20.0 (a total of 410 incidents). In 2005, BLS conducted another survey specifically

on workplace violence prevention.[2] In this survey, BLS asked employers about their establishments' operations, programs and policies regarding workplace violence. These survey results showed that while 4.8% of all private industry establishments reported experiencing some form of workplace violence, 7.1% of employers from the retail trade reported experiencing such an incident. Retail trade establishments which did experience such incidents also reported having higher rates of absenteeism due to these incidents than did all private industry establishments. Surprisingly, while 28.3% of retail trade employers reported that such incidents had negative impacts on workers, only 1.9% reported changing their program or policy after an incident occurred.

According to an earlier survey conducted by the U.S. Bureau of Justice Statistics (BJS), retail sales occupations had the third highest victimization rate, after workers in the law enforcement and mental health professions. The BJS National Crime Victimization Survey (1993-1999) found that 20 out of 1,000 workers in retail had experienced some form of simple or aggravated assault in the workplace annually, and the rate for convenience store and gas station workers was much higher. Their rate was 53.9 and 68.3 per 1,000 workers, respectively. In addition, 21% of all workplace robberies involved personnel in retail sales.

The risk factors
A number of factors put late-night retail workers at risk. These include:

- The exchange of money (making them targets for robbery);
- Solo work and isolated work sites;
- The sale of alcohol;
- Poorly lit stores and parking areas; and
- Lack of staff training in recognizing and managing escalating hostile and aggressive behavior.

An Effective Violence Prevention Program
In January 1989, OSHA published voluntary, generic safety and health program management guidelines,[3] followed by recommendations for work-

---

[1] Incidence rates for non-fatal injuries and illnesses involving days away from work is defined as the number of incidents per 10,000 full-time workers.

[2] BLS conducted this voluntary survey for the National Institute for Occupational Safety and Health and the Centers for Disease Control and Prevention. The *Survey of Workplace Violence Prevention* looked at the prevalence of security features, the risks facing workers, employer policies and training, and related topics associated with maintaining a safe work environment.

[3] OSHA's *Safety and Health Program Management Guidelines; Issuance of Voluntary Guidelines*, 54 Fed. Reg. 3904-3916, January 26, 1989.

OSHA
Occupational Safety and
Health Administration

place violence prevention programs in late-night retail establishments, published in 1998.[4] The violence prevention information presented in this document builds on those guidelines by identifying risk factors and describing some feasible solutions. Although not exhaustive, these workplace violence guidelines include policy recommendations and practical corrective methods to help prevent and mitigate the effects of workplace violence in late-night retail establishments.

The goal of this document is to encourage employers to implement programs to identify the potential risks of workplace violence and to implement corrective measures. These recommendations are not a "model program" or a rigid package of violence prevention steps uniformly applicable to all establishments. No single strategy is appropriate for all businesses, since environmental and other risk factors for workplace violence differ widely among workplaces. Employers may use a combination of strategies recommended in this document, as appropriate, for their particular workplace.

While OSHA encourages employers to develop a written program for workplace violence prevention,

the extent to which the components of the program are in writing is less important than how effective the program is in practice. By implementing appropriate hazard prevention and control measures, and ensuring management and worker involvement, employers will take the most critical steps in protecting their workplace from violent acts. A written statement of policy serves as a touchstone for the many separate plans, procedures and actions required for an effective prevention program. In smaller establishments, a program can be effective without being documented. As the size of a workplace or the complexity of hazard control increases, written guidance becomes more important as a way to ensure clear communication and consistent application of policies and procedures. An employer could create a separate workplace violence prevention program or incorporate this information into an existing accident prevention program, employee handbook, or manual of standard operating procedures.

These recommendations are not a new standard or regulation and do not create any new OSHA duties. Therefore, these recommendations are not intended to establish a legal standard of care with respect to workplace violence. Accordingly, these recommendations do not impose any new legal obligations or constraints on employers or the states.

---

[4] OSHA's *Recommendations for Workplace Violence Prevention Programs in Late-Night Retail Establishments, OSHA Publication 3153, 1998.*

Violence Prevention Programs

Violence prevention programs should set clear goals and objectives to prevent workplace violence. The goals and objectives must be suitable for the size and complexity of workplace operations. In addition, the program should be adaptable to different situations at the worksite. Whatever format the program takes, it is critical that employers clearly explain the prevention program to all workers.

At a minimum, workplace violence prevention programs should:

- Establish a clear policy for workplace violence, verbal and nonverbal threats and related actions. All personnel employed in the retail establishment should know the policy.

- Ensure that no worker who reports or experiences workplace violence faces reprisals.[5]

- Encourage workers to promptly report incidents and suggest ways to reduce or eliminate risks. Require records of incidents to assess risk and measure progress.

- Outline a comprehensive plan for maintaining security in the workplace. The plan should include establishing a liaison with law enforcement representatives and others who can help identify ways to prevent and mitigate workplace violence.

- Assign responsibility and authority for the program to individuals or teams with appropriate training and skills. Ensure that adequate resources are available and that those responsible for the program develop expertise on workplace violence prevention in late-night retail settings.

- Affirm management commitment to an environment that places as much importance on worker safety and health as on serving store patrons.

Elements of an Effective Violence Prevention Program

The four components of an effective safety and health management system also apply to the prevention of workplace violence, and are:

- Management commitment and worker involvement;

- Worksite analysis;

- Hazard prevention and control; and

- Safety and health training.

Management Commitment and Worker Involvement

Management commitment and worker involvement are complementary and essential elements of an effective safety and health management system. To ensure an effective program, management and frontline workers must work together. If employers opt to use a team or committee approach to addressing this element they must be careful to comply with the applicable provisions of the *National Labor Relations Act.*[6]

Management Commitment

By obligating resources – both human capital and financial – management provides the motivation and ability to effectively address workplace violence. Management commitment should include:

- Demonstrating organizational concern for worker emotional and physical safety and health, which includes medical and psychological counseling and debriefing for personnel who experience or witness assaults and other violent incidents;

- Exhibiting equal commitment to the safety and health of workers and store patrons;

- Assigning responsibility for the various aspects of the workplace violence prevention program to ensure that all managers, supervisors and workers understand their obligations;

- Allocating appropriate authority and resources to all responsible parties;

- Maintaining a system of accountability for involved managers, supervisors and workers;

- Supporting and implementing appropriate recommendations from safety and health committees; and

- Working constructively with other parties, such as landlords, lessees, local police and other public safety agencies to improve security in and around the worksite.

Worker Involvement

Worker involvement in violence prevention is especially critical in the late-night retail setting.

---

[5] Section 11(c)(1) of the OSH Act applies to protected activity involving hazards of workplace violence as it does for other health and safety matters: "No person shall discharge or in any manner discriminate against any employee because such employee has filed any complaint or instituted or caused to be instituted any proceedings under or related to this Act or has testified or is about to testify in any such proceeding or because of the exercise by such employee on behalf of himself or others of any right afforded by this Act."

[6] 29 U.S.C. 158(a)(2) stipulates that an employer can ask that an employee confer but without loss of time or pay.

OSHA
Occupational Safety and
Health Administration

Frontline workers are often the most knowledgeable of business procedures and the business environment – especially in situations where no manager is on duty. Workers' experiences can help to identify practical solutions to safety challenges. The more inclusive the approach to developing a workplace violence prevention plan, the more comprehensive it will be. In addition, workers who are engaged in violence prevention programs are more likely to support them and ensure their effectiveness.

Workers should be involved by:
- Contributing to the development of procedures that address safety and security concerns, including responding to surveys on these issues;
- Understanding and complying with the workplace violence prevention program and safety and security measures;
- Reporting violent incidents promptly and accurately;
- Participating in safety and health committees or teams that receive reports of violent incidents or security problems, make facility inspections and respond with recommendations for corrective strategies; and
- Taking part in training programs and sharing on-the-job experiences that cover techniques to recognize escalating agitation, aggressive behavior or criminal intent.

Worksite Analysis

A worksite analysis involves a step-by-step assessment to identify environmental and operational risks for violence. The analysis entails reviewing specific procedures or operations that contribute to hazards, identifying areas where hazards may develop and performing periodic safety audits. Since the hazard analysis is the foundation for the violence prevention program, it is important for the employer to carefully consider the person(s) or team that will conduct the analysis. If a team is used, it should include representatives from senior management, operations, workers, security, occupational safety and health personnel, legal and human resources staff. A small business may only need to assign the duty to a single worker or consultant.

The recommended program for worksite analysis includes, but is not limited to:
- Analyzing and tracking records;
- Conducting screening surveys; and
- Analyzing workplace security.

Records Review and Analysis

To begin a hazard analysis an employer should review previous business experiences for at least two or three years. The employer should collect and examine any medical, safety, workers' compensation and insurance records to identify any incidents of workplace violence. The review should include the OSHA Log of Work-Related Injuries and Illnesses (OSHA Form 300), if the employer is required to maintain one.[7] In addition, worker and police reports of incidents or near-incidents of assaults or aggressive behavior should be examined to identify and analyze trends in assaults relative to particular:
- Job titles;
- Workstations; and
- Date and time of day.

Through this analysis, an employer can identify the frequency and severity of incidents to establish a baseline for measuring improvement. Employers with more than one store or worksite may review each location's history of violence. To learn about trends in the community or industry an employer may contact local businesses, trade associations, police departments and community and civic groups. An employer should use several years of data, if possible, to gain a clear understanding of the existing trends.

Conducting Screening Surveys

Finding few documented cases of workplace violence should not be dismissed as random, because incidents may go unreported or undocumented. Management may not be aware of low intensity incidents or threats of violence that workers experienced. A worker questionnaire or survey about workplace violence issues can identify:
- If customers have assaulted workers;
- If the business has had to address other crimes, such as shoplifting;
- If workers have been threatened or harassed while on duty;
- Whether firearms were carried and/or used;
- How many workers were on duty when incidents occurred;
- Whether police were called;

---

[7] 29 CFR Part 1904.1 exempts employers with 10 or fewer employees at all times during a calendar year from maintaining an OSHA injury and illness log. In addition, 29 CFR 1904.2 exempts businesses classified in specific low-hazard retail, service, finance, insurance, or real estate industry from keeping these injury and illness records.

- What workers were doing before and during the incident;
- Whether preventive measures were in place at the time of the incident and whether they were implemented;
- Where incidents occurred; and
- How often these incidents occurred.

Employers may also use surveys to solicit workers' ideas on the potential for violent incidents and to identify or confirm the need for improved security measures. Detailed baseline screening surveys can help pinpoint tasks that put workers at risk. Periodic surveys, conducted at least annually or when business operations change or workplace violence incidents occur, can help employers identify new or previously unnoticed risk factors in work practices, procedures or controls. After these reviews, employers should provide feedback and follow-up with their workers.

Employers may choose to use independent reviewers to conduct and analyze these surveys. Independent reviewers, such as safety and health professionals, law enforcement/security specialists and insurance safety auditors, may offer advice to strengthen programs. These experts can also provide fresh perspectives to improve a violence prevention program.

Workplace Security Analysis

Employers should have the designated team, worker or consultant periodically inspect the worksite and evaluate job tasks to identify hazards, conditions, operations and situations that could expose workers to violence. An initial walkthrough survey should be conducted to identify risks and establish a baseline. To find areas requiring further evaluation, the team or coordinator should:

- Analyze incidents, including the characteristics of assailants and victims. Incident descriptions should include an account of what happened before and during the incident, and the relevant details of the situation and its outcome. When possible, someone should obtain police reports and recommendations.
- Identify jobs or locations with the greatest risk of violence as well as processes and procedures that put workers at risk of assault. The analysis should include an estimate of the frequency and time when the risk of violence is greatest.
- Note high risk factors such as types of store patrons or environmental factors, such as: building layouts, interior and exterior lighting, com-

munication systems (such as telephones), and where security systems are installed.

- Evaluate the effectiveness of existing security measures, including engineering controls. Analysis should include whether or not security measures are being implemented and whether or not they reduce or eliminate risk factors. If security measures are not being implemented, the analysis should determine what has inhibited their use.

Appendix A contains some sample checklists that may assist employers in developing their own security analyses. Trade associations and other organizations may also have materials that can assist employers in assessing the risk of violent incidents at their worksites. In addition, some local law enforcement agencies provide free advice to business owners on ways to reduce exposure to crime. As with the workplace surveys, employers may choose to hire independent consultants to analyze their worksites for security weaknesses.

Hazard Prevention and Control

By effectively preventing and controlling workplace violence hazards, employers are better able to protect workers and avoid workplace incidents. After hazards are identified through the systematic worksite analysis, employers will need to take steps to prevent or control those hazards. Employers or someone they designate should develop measures that include engineering, procedural, and/or administrative changes to reduce or eliminate the likelihood of violent incidents. Employers will likely need to use a combination of controls to manage the hazards identified through their hazard analyses but should carefully assess the effectiveness of each type of approach. Engineering controls are considered the most effective because they make physical improvements without any dependence on human behavior. If a given situation does not allow for engineering controls, employers should next consider procedural and administrative changes. Once prevention and control measures are in place, employers should ensure that procedures are followed and that workers are supported.

Minimizing Risk through Engineering Controls and Workplace Adaptations

Engineering controls remove the hazard from the workplace or create a barrier between the worker and the hazard. Several measures, such as those described in the following paragraphs, can effectively prevent or control workplace hazards at retail establishments. The selection of any measure should be based on the hazards identified in the workplace security analysis.

Given that late-night retail businesses are prone to robberies, employers should seek to reduce their risk by improving visibility and surveillance, controlling customers' access, and limiting the availability of cash. Such measures could include:

- Limiting window signs to low or high locations and keeping shelving low so that workers can see incoming customers and so that police can observe what is occurring from the outside of the store;

- Ensuring the customer service and cash register areas are visible from outside the establishment;

- Placing curved mirrors at hallway intersections or concealed areas;

- Maintaining adequate lighting inside and outside the establishment;

- Installing video surveillance equipment and closed circuit TV to increase the likelihood of identification of perpetrators;

- Using door detectors so that workers are alerted when someone enters the store;

- Having height markers on exit doors to help witnesses provide more accurate descriptions of assailants;

- Installing and regularly maintaining alarm systems and other security devices, panic buttons, handheld alarms or noise devices, cellular phones and private channel radios where risk is apparent or may be anticipated;

- Arranging for a reliable response system when an alarm is triggered;

- Installing fences and other structures to direct the flow of customer traffic into and around the store;

- Controlling access to the store with door entry (buzzer) systems;

- Installing physical barriers such as bullet-resistant enclosures with pass-through windows between customers and workers; and

- Using drop safes to limit the availability of cash to cashiers and posting signs which state that cashiers have limited access to cash.

Minimizing Risk through Administrative and Work Practice Controls

Administrative and work practice controls affect the way workers perform their jobs or specific tasks. Changes in work practices and administrative pro-

cedures can help prevent violent incidents. Often policies are needed to ensure that the engineering controls are implemented and used effectively. For example, employers should:

- Integrate violence prevention activities into daily procedures, such as checking lighting, locks, and security cameras to help maintain a secure worksite.

- Require workers to use the drop safes and keep a minimal amount of cash in each register.

- Develop and implement procedures for the correct use of physical barriers, such as enclosures and pass-through windows.

- Establish a policy of when doors should be locked. Require workers to keep doors locked before and after official business hours. Require workers to lock doors used for deliveries and garbage removal when not in use. In addition, require that deliveries be made during normal daytime operations.

- Develop and implement emergency procedures for workers to use in case of a robbery or security breach – such as calling the police or triggering an alarm.

Other administrative and work practice controls, independent of engineering controls include:

- Prohibit transactions with large bills (over $20). If this is not practical because of frequent transactions over $20, cash levels should be kept as low as practical. Workers should not carry business receipts on their persons unless it is absolutely necessary.

- When possible, increase staffing levels at stores with a history of robbery or assaults, or located in high crime areas. Use the "buddy system," especially when personal safety may be threatened.

- Establish rules and practices to ensure that workers can walk to garbage areas and outdoor storage areas without increasing their risk of assault.

- Establish liaison with local police and state prosecutors. Report all incidents of violence. Give police physical layouts of facilities to expedite investigations.

- Require workers to report all assaults or threats to a supervisor or manager (for example, through a confidential interview). Keep log books and reports of such incidents to help determine any necessary actions to prevent recurrences.

- Advise workers of company procedures for requesting police assistance or filing charges when assaulted if necessary.

- Provide management support during emergencies. Respond promptly to all complaints.

- Set up a trained response team to respond to emergencies.

- Use properly trained security officers to deal with aggressive behavior. Follow written security procedures.

- Discourage workers from wearing necklaces or chains to help prevent possible strangulation in confrontational situations.

- Provide staff members with security escorts to parking areas in evening or late hours. Ensure that parking areas are highly visible, well lit and safely accessible to the building.

Administrative controls work only if they are followed. Employers should monitor workers regularly to ensure that proper work practices are being used. Employers should also provide periodic constructive feedback to workers to ensure that they understand and appreciate the importance of these procedures.

Employer Responses to Incidents of Violence

Post-incident responses and evaluations are essential for an effective violence prevention program. Policies should include standard operating procedures for management and workers to follow in the aftermath of a violent incident. Response procedures should ensure that the incident is properly investigated, workers receive the appropriate attention and, in the event of injury, injured workers receive prompt and appropriate medical treatment. Such procedures may include the following:

- Providing prompt first aid and emergency medical treatment for injured workers, which may include transportation to the local emergency medical facility.

- Reporting incidents to the police or notifying other authorities as required by applicable laws and regulations.[8]

- Securing the premises to safeguard evidence and reduce distractions during the post-incident response process so that police or authorities may investigate properly.

- Preparing an incident report immediately after the incident, noting details that might be forgot-

ten over time. Appendix B contains sample incident report forms that an employer may use or adapt.

- Informing management about the incident.

Victims of workplace violence suffer a variety of consequences, in addition to their actual physical injuries. These may include:

- Short- and long-term psychological trauma;

- Fear of returning to work;

- Changes in relationships with coworkers and family;

- Feelings of incompetence, guilt, powerlessness; and

- Fear of criticism by supervisors or managers.

Consequently, a strong follow-up program for these workers will not only help them to deal with these problems, but also help prepare them to confront or prevent future incidents of violence.

Several types of assistance can be incorporated into the post-incident response. For example, trauma crisis counseling, critical incident stress debriefing or employee assistance programs may be provided to assist victims. Certified employee assistance professionals, psychologists, psychiatrists, clinical nurse specialists or social workers may provide this counseling or the employer may refer workers to an outside specialist. In addition, the employer may establish an employee counseling service, peer counseling or support groups.

Counselors should be well trained and have a good understanding of the issues and consequences of assaults and other aggressive, violent behavior. Appropriate and promptly rendered post-incident debriefings and counseling reduce acute psychological trauma and general stress levels among victims and witnesses. In addition, this type of counseling educates staff about workplace violence and positively influences workplace and organizational cultural norms to reduce trauma associated with future incidents.

Safety and Health Training

Training and education ensure that all staff members are aware of potential security hazards and how to protect themselves and their coworkers through established policies and procedures. Workers with different jobs and responsibilities may need different types and levels of training.

Training for All Employees

Every employee, including supervisors and managers, should understand the concept of "universal

---

[8] As required by 29 CFR 1904.39(a), all employers must report to OSHA, within eight hours, a fatality resulting from a workplace incident or the hospitalization of three or more employees resulting from a workplace incident.

precautions for violence,"[9] which refers to the concept that violence should be expected but can be avoided or mitigated through proper precautionary preparation. Workers need to know the specific hazards associated with their jobs and worksite to help them minimize their risk of assault and injury. Training should include information on worksite-specific potential hazards and instructions on how to control those hazards. Training should also include guidance to limit workers from intervening in workplace altercations whenever possible unless enough staff or emergency response teams and security personnel are available. Topics may include the following:

- An overview of the potential risk of assault;
- The workplace violence prevention policy;
- Operational procedures, such as cash handling rules, designed to reduce risk;
- Proper use of security measures and engineering controls designed to reduce risk;
- Early recognition of escalating behavior or recognition of warning signs of situations that may lead to assaults;
- Behavioral strategies such as conflict resolution and aggression management techniques to defuse tense situations and reduce the likelihood of a violent outcome;
- The location and operation of safety devices such as alarm systems, along with required maintenance schedules and procedures;
- Policies and procedures for reporting the incident to the proper authorities, as well as record-keeping;
- Policies and procedures for obtaining medical care, counseling, workers' compensation or legal assistance after a violent episode or injury;
- Specific instructions on how to respond to a robbery such as turning over money or valuables without resistance, and how to respond to attempted shoplifting; and
- Emergency action procedures to be followed in the event of a robbery or violent incident.

Qualified trainers should provide instruction at the comprehension level appropriate for workers. Effective training programs involve role-playing, simulations and drills. At a minimum, employers should provide required training annually. Workers

---

[9] The concept of "universal precautions" began in the medical field and refers to the practice of assuming that all patients are infectious and therefore requires avoiding contact with patients' bodily fluids by means of wearing the appropriate personal protective equipment.

who forget safety measures should be retrained. New, reassigned, temporary and visiting workers should receive the same training as permanent staff. In addition, establishments with high worker turnover may need to provide training more frequently.

The training program should also include an evaluation. At least annually, the team or coordinator responsible for the program should review its content, methods and the frequency of training. Program evaluations may involve supervisor and worker interviews, testing, observing, and reviewing reports of behavior of individuals in threatening situations.

Training for Supervisors/Managers and Security Personnel

Supervisors and managers need to recognize high-risk situations, so they can ensure that workers are not placed in assignments that compromise their safety. Following training, supervisors and managers should be able to recognize a potentially hazardous situation and to make any necessary changes in the physical worksite and/or policies and procedures to reduce or eliminate hazards. They should also be able to handle traumatized workers.

Security personnel need specific training relating to the worksite, including the psychological components of handling aggressive and abusive store patrons, and ways to handle aggression and defuse hostile situations.

Recordkeeping and Program Evaluations

Recordkeeping and evaluations of the violence prevention program are necessary to determine its overall effectiveness and identify any deficiencies.

Records Employers Should Maintain

Recordkeeping is essential to the program's success. Good records help employers determine the severity of the problem, evaluate methods of hazard control and identify training needs. Records can be especially useful to large organizations and members of a business group or trade association who "pool" data. Through trend analysis, records of injuries, illnesses, accidents, assaults, hazards, corrective actions, histories and training can help identify problems and solutions for an effective program.

Employers can tailor their recordkeeping practices to the needs of their violence prevention program. Maintaining records enables employers to monitor ongoing efforts to deter workplace violence, to determine if a violence prevention program is working and to identify ways to improve it.

Important records employers may maintain include:

- OSHA Log of Work-Related Injuries and Illnesses (OSHA Form 300). Employers who are required to keep this log must record any new work-related injury that results in death, days away from work, days of restriction or job transfer, medical treatment beyond first aid, loss of consciousness or a significant injury diagnosed by a licensed healthcare professional. Injuries caused by assaults must be entered on the log if they meet the recording criteria.

- Medical reports of work injury and supervisors' reports for each recorded assault. These records should describe the type of assault, such as an unprovoked sudden attack or patron-to-patron altercation; who was assaulted; and all other circumstances of the incident. The records should include a description of the environment or location, potential or actual cost, lost work time that resulted and the nature of injuries sustained. These medical records are confidential documents and should be kept in a locked location under the direct responsibility of a healthcare professional.

- Records of incidents of abuse, verbal attacks or aggressive behavior that may be threatening, such as pushing or shouting and acts of aggression toward other clients. These records may be kept as part of an incident report. Employers should ensure that the affected department evaluates these records routinely. (See sample violence incident forms in Appendix B.)

- Documentation of minutes of safety meetings, records of hazard analyses and corrective actions recommended and taken.

- Records of all training programs, attendees and qualification of trainers.

Program Evaluation Elements
As part of their overall program, employers should evaluate their safety and security measures. Top management should review the program regularly, and with each incident, evaluate its success. Responsible parties (including managers, supervisors and workers) should reevaluate policies and procedures on a regular basis to identify deficiencies and take corrective action.

Management should share workplace violence prevention evaluation reports with all workers. Any changes in the programs should be discussed at regular meetings of the safety committee, and with union representatives or other worker groups.

All reports should protect worker confidentiality either by presenting only aggregate data or by removing personal identifiers if individual data are used.

The processes involved in an evaluation should include:

- Establishing a uniform violence reporting system and regular review of reports;

- Reviewing reports and minutes from staff meetings on safety and security issues;

- Analyzing trends and rates in injuries, illnesses or fatalities caused by violence relative to initial or "baseline" rates;

- Measuring improvement based on lowering the frequency and severity of workplace violence;

- Keeping up-to-date records of administrative and work practice changes to prevent workplace violence and to evaluate how well they work;

- Surveying workers before and after making job or worksite changes or installing security measures or new systems to determine their effectiveness;

- Keeping abreast of new strategies available to address violence in retail establishments, as they develop;

- Complying with OSHA and State requirements for recording and reporting injuries, illnesses and deaths; and

- Requesting periodic law enforcement or outside consultant review of the worksite for recommendations on improving worker safety.

Conclusion

Workplace violence has emerged as a major occupational safety and health issue in many industries,
especially the retail trade. OSHA's voluntary recommendations offer systematic frameworks to help
employers protect workers from risks of injury and
death from occupationally-related violence. By treating workplace violence as a preventable hazard,
employers can develop practical, effective strategies
to protect their workers from this serious risk and
provide a safe, healthful working environment.

Appendices

Appendix A:
Sample Workplace Violence Factors and Control Checklists

These sample checklists can help employers identify present or potential workplace violence problems. They contain various factors and controls that are commonly encountered in retail establishments.

Not all of the questions listed here fit all types of retail businesses, and these checklists obviously do not include all possible topics specific businesses need. Employers should expand, modify, and adapt these checklists to fit their own circumstances. These suggestions are not new regulations or standards, and the fact that an employer does not adopt a listed control does not prove a violation of the General Duty clause. ("N/A" stands for "not applicable").

Sample Checklist 1:

Yes	No	N/A	**Environmental Factors**
			Do workers exchange money with the public?
			Is the business open during evening or late-night hours?
			Is the site located in a high crime area?
			Has the site experienced a robbery in the past 3 years?
			Has the site experienced other violent acts in the past 3 years?
			Has the site experienced threats, harassment, or other abusive behavior in the past 3 years?
Yes	No	N/A	**Engineering Controls**
			Do workers have access to a telephone with an outside line?
			Are emergency telephone numbers for law enforcement, fire and medical services, and an internal contact person posted next to the phone?
			Are emergency telephone numbers programmed into company telephones?
			Is the entrance to the building easily seen from the street and free of heavy shrub growth?
			Is lighting bright in outside, parking and adjacent areas?
			Are windows and views outside and inside clear of advertising or other obstructions?
			Is the cash register in plain view of customers and police cruisers to deter robberies?
			Is there a working drop safe or time access safe to minimize cash on hand?
			Are security cameras and mirrors placed in locations that would deter robbers or provide greater security for employees?
			Are there height markers on exit doors to help witnesses provide more complete descriptions of assailants?
			Are employees protected through the use of bullet-resistant enclosures in locations with a history of robberies or assaults in a high crime area?
Yes	No	N/A	**Administrative/Work Practice Controls**
			Are there emergency procedures in place to address robberies and other acts of potential violence?
			Have workers been instructed to report suspicious persons or activities?
			Are workers trained in emergency response procedures for robberies and other crimes that may occur on the premises?

Occupational Safety and
Health Administration

Yes	No	N/A	Administrative/Work Practice Controls (*continued*)
			Are workers trained in conflict resolution and in nonviolent response to threatening situations?
			Is cash control a key element of the establishment's violence and robbery prevention program?
			Does the site have a policy limiting the number of cash registers open during late-night hours?
			Does the site have a policy to maintain less than $50 in the cash register? (This may not be possible in stores that have lottery tickets and payouts.)
			Are signs posted notifying the public that limited cash, no drugs, and no other valuables are kept on the premises?
			Do workers have at least one other person throughout their shifts, or are other protective measures utilized when workers are working alone in locations with a history of robberies or assaults in a high crime area?
			Are there procedures in place to assure the safety of workers who open and close the store?

Sample Checklist 2 – Self Inspection Security Checklist:
Reprinted with permission of the Hartford Financial Services Group, Inc., *Workplace Violence Prevention Program Loss Control TIPS* – Technical Information Paper Series

Facility: _____

Inspector: _____

Date of Inspection: _____

Security Control Plan?	❑ **Yes**	❑ **No**
If yes, does it contain:		
Policy Statement?	❑ Yes	❑ No
Review of Worker Incident Exposure?	❑ Yes	❑ No
Methods of Control?	❑ Yes	❑ No
If yes, does it include:		
Engineering	❑ Yes	❑ No
Work practice	❑ Yes	❑ No
Training	❑ Yes	❑ No
Reporting procedures	❑ Yes	❑ No
Recordkeeping	❑ Yes	❑ No
Counseling	❑ Yes	❑ No
Evaluation of incidents?	❑ Yes	❑ No
Floor Plan?	❑ Yes	❑ No
Protection of Assets?	❑ Yes	❑ No
Computer Security?	❑ Yes	❑ No
Plan accessible to all workers?	❑ Yes	❑ No
Plan reviewed and updated annually?	❑ Yes	❑ No
Plan reviewed and updated when tasks added or changed?	❑ Yes	❑ No
Policy statement by employer?	❑ **Yes**	❑ **No**
Work areas evaluated by employer?	❑ **Yes**	❑ **No**
If yes, how often? _____		
Engineering controls?	❑ **Yes**	❑ **No**
If yes, does it include:		
Mirrors to see around corners and in blind spots?	❑ Yes	❑ No
Landscaping to provide unobstructed view of the workplace?	❑ Yes	❑ No
"Fishbowl effect" to allow unobstructed view of the interior?	❑ Yes	❑ No
Limiting the posting of sale signs on windows?	❑ Yes	❑ No
Adequate lighting in and around the workplace?	❑ Yes	❑ No
Parking lot well lighted?	❑ Yes	❑ No
Door control(s)?	❑ Yes	❑ No
Panic button(s)?	❑ Yes	❑ No
Door detector(s)?	❑ Yes	❑ No
Closed circuit TV?	❑ Yes	❑ No

OSHA®
Occupational Safety and
Health Administration

Stationary metal detector?	☐ Yes	☐ No
Sound detection?	☐ Yes	☐ No
Intrusion detection system?	☐ Yes	☐ No
Intrusion panel?	☐ Yes	☐ No
Monitor(s)?	☐ Yes	☐ No
Videotape recorder?	☐ Yes	☐ No
Switcher?	☐ Yes	☐ No
Handheld metal detector?	☐ Yes	☐ No
Handheld video camera?	☐ Yes	☐ No
Personnel traps ("Sally Traps")?	☐ Yes	☐ No
Other?	☐ Yes	☐ No

Structural modifications

Plexiglas, glass guard, wire glass, partitions, etc.?	☐ **Yes**	☐ **No**

If yes, comment: _____

Security guards? ☐ **Yes** ☐ **No**

If yes, are there an appropriate number for the site?	☐ Yes	☐ No
Are they knowledgeable of the company WPVP Policy?	☐ Yes	☐ No

Indicate if they are:

_____ Contract Guards (1)

_____ In-house Workers (2)

At Entrance(s)?	☐ Yes	☐ No
Building Patrol?	☐ Yes	☐ No
Guards provided with communication?	☐ Yes	☐ No

If yes, indicate what type: _____

Guards receive training on Workplace Violence situations?	☐ Yes	☐ No

Comments: _____

_____

Work practice controls? ☐ **Yes** ☐ **No**

If yes, indicate:

Desks clear of objects which may become missiles?	☐ Yes	☐ No
Unobstructed office exits?	☐ Yes	☐ No
Vacant (Bare) cubicles available?	☐ Yes	☐ No
Reception area available?	☐ Yes	☐ No
Visitor/client sign in/out?	☐ Yes	☐ No
Visitor(s)/client(s) escorted?	☐ Yes	☐ No
One entrance used?	☐ Yes	☐ No
Separate interview area(s)?	☐ Yes	☐ No

I.D. badges used?	☐ Yes	☐ No
Emergency numbers posted by phones?	☐ Yes	☐ No
Internal phone system?	☐ Yes	☐ No
If yes, indicate:		
Does it use 120 VAC building lines?	☐ Yes	☐ No
Does it use phone lines?	☐ Yes	☐ No
Internal procedures for conflict (problem) situations?	☐ Yes	☐ No
Procedures for worker dismissal?	☐ Yes	☐ No
Limit spouse & family visits to designated areas?	☐ Yes	☐ No
Key control procedures?	☐ Yes	☐ No
Access control to the workplace?	☐ Yes	☐ No
Objects which may become missiles removed from area?	☐ Yes	☐ No
Parking prohibited in fire zones?	☐ Yes	☐ No

Other:_____

_____

OSHA
Occupational Safety and
Health Administration

Sample Checklist 3 – Workplace Violence Inspection Checklist:
This checklist was adapted from *Violence on the Job: A Guidebook for Labor and Management*, published by the Labor Occupational Health Program, University of California, Berkeley.

Staffing

Is there someone responsible for building security?
❏ Yes ❏ No ❏ Sometimes Notes _____
Who is it? _____

Are workers told who is responsible for security?
❏ Yes ❏ No ❏ Sometimes Notes _____

Is adequate and trained staffing available to protect workers against assaults or other violence?
❏ Yes ❏ No ❏ Sometimes Notes _____

Is there a "buddy system" to use when workers are in potentially dangerous situations?
❏ Yes ❏ No ❏ Sometimes Notes _____

Are there trained security personnel accessible to workers in a timely manner?
❏ Yes ❏ No ❏ Sometimes Notes _____

Do security personnel have sufficient authority to take all necessary action to ensure worker safety?
❏ Yes ❏ No ❏ Sometimes Notes _____

Are security personnel provided outside the building?
❏ Yes ❏ No ❏ Sometimes Notes _____

Is the parking lot attended or otherwise secure?
❏ Yes ❏ No ❏ Sometimes Notes _____

Are security escorts available to walk workers to and from the parking lot?
❏ Yes ❏ No ❏ Sometimes Notes _____

Training

Are workers trained in the emergency response plan (for example, escape routes, notifying the proper authorities)?
❏ Yes ❏ No ❏ Sometimes Notes _____

Are workers trained to report violent incidents or threats?
❏ Yes ❏ No ❏ Sometimes Notes _____

Are workers trained in how to handle difficult customers?
❏ Yes ❏ No ❏ Sometimes Notes _____

Are workers trained in ways to prevent or defuse potentially violent situations?
❏ Yes   ❏ No   ❏ Sometimes   Notes _____

Are workers trained in personal safety and self-defense?
❏ Yes   ❏ No   ❏ Sometimes   Notes _____

Facility Design
Are there enough exits and adequate routes of escape?
❏ Yes   ❏ No   ❏ Sometimes   Notes _____

Can exit doors be opened only from the inside to prevent unauthorized entry?
❏ Yes   ❏ No   ❏ Sometimes   Notes _____

Is the lighting adequate to see clearly in indoor areas?
❏ Yes   ❏ No   ❏ Sometimes   Notes _____

Are there worker-only work areas that are separate from public areas?
❏ Yes   ❏ No   ❏ Sometimes   Notes _____

Is a secure place available for workers to store their personal belongings?
❏ Yes   ❏ No   ❏ Sometimes   Notes _____

Are private, locked restrooms available for staff?
❏ Yes   ❏ No   ❏ Sometimes   Notes _____

Security Measures
Does the workplace have:
Physical barriers (Plexiglas partitions, elevated counters to prevent people from jumping over them, bulletproof customer windows, etc.)?
❏ Yes   ❏ No   ❏ Sometimes   Notes _____

Security cameras or closed-circuit TV in high risk areas?
❏ Yes   ❏ No   ❏ Sometimes   Notes _____

Panic buttons (portable or fixed)?
❏ Yes   ❏ No   ❏ Sometimes   Notes _____

Alarm systems?
❏ Yes   ❏ No   ❏ Sometimes   Notes _____

Internal phone system to activate emergency assistance?
❏ Yes   ❏ No   ❏ Sometimes   Notes _____

Phones with an outside line programmed to call 911?
❏ Yes   ❏ No   ❏ Sometimes   Notes _____

⊙SHA®
Occupational Safety and
Health Administration

Two-way radios, pagers or cellular phones?
❏ Yes　　❏ No　　❏ Sometimes　　Notes _____

Security mirrors (convex mirrors)?
❏ Yes　　❏ No　　❏ Sometimes　　Notes _____

Secured entry (buzzers)?
❏ Yes　　❏ No　　❏ Sometimes　　Notes _____

Personal alarm devices?
❏ Yes　　❏ No　　❏ Sometimes　　Notes _____

Outside The Facility
Do workers feel safe walking to and from the workplace?
❏ Yes　　❏ No　　❏ Sometimes　　Notes _____

Are the entrances to the building clearly visible from the street?
❏ Yes　　❏ No　　❏ Sometimes　　Notes _____

Is the area surrounding the building free of bushes or other hiding places?
❏ Yes　　❏ No　　❏ Sometimes　　Notes _____

Is video surveillance provided outside the building?
❏ Yes　　❏ No　　❏ Sometimes　　Notes _____

Is there enough lighting to see clearly outside the building?
❏ Yes　　❏ No　　❏ Sometimes　　Notes _____

Are all exterior walkways visible to security personnel?
❏ Yes　　❏ No　　❏ Sometimes　　Notes _____

Is there a nearby parking lot reserved for workers only?
❏ Yes　　❏ No　　❏ Sometimes　　Notes _____

Is the parking lot free of bushes or other hiding places?
❏ Yes　　❏ No　　❏ Sometimes　　Notes _____

Is there enough lighting to see clearly in the parking lot and when walking to the building?
❏ Yes　　❏ No　　❏ Sometimes　　Notes _____

Have neighboring facilities and businesses experienced violence or crime?
❏ Yes　　❏ No　　❏ Sometimes　　Notes _____

Workplace Procedures

Is public access to the building controlled?
☐ Yes ☐ No ☐ Sometimes Notes _____

Are floor plans posted showing building entrances, exits?
☐ Yes ☐ No ☐ Sometimes Notes _____

Are these floor plans visible only to staff and not to outsiders?
☐ Yes ☐ No ☐ Sometimes Notes _____

Is other emergency information posted, such as telephone numbers?
☐ Yes ☐ No ☐ Sometimes Notes _____

Are special security measures taken to protect people who work late at night (escorts, locked entrances, etc.)?
☐ Yes ☐ No ☐ Sometimes Notes _____

Are authorized visitors to the building required to wear ID badges?
☐ Yes ☐ No ☐ Sometimes Notes _____

Are identification tags required for staff (omitting personal information such as the person's last name and Social Security number)?
☐ Yes ☐ No ☐ Sometimes Notes _____

Are workers notified of past violent activity?
☐ Yes ☐ No ☐ Sometimes Notes _____

Is there an established liaison with local police?
☐ Yes ☐ No ☐ Sometimes Notes _____

Are broken windows and locks repaired promptly?
☐ Yes ☐ No ☐ Sometimes Notes _____

Are security devices (locks, cameras, alarms, etc.) tested on a regular basis and repaired promptly when necessary?
☐ Yes ☐ No ☐ Sometimes Notes _____

Field Work

Staffing:

Is there adequate staffing in the establishment?
☐ Yes ☐ No ☐ Sometimes Notes _____

Are escorts or "buddies" provided for people who work in potentially dangerous situations?
☐ Yes ☐ No ☐ Sometimes Notes _____

Training:
Are workers briefed about the area in which they will be working (gang colors, neighborhood culture, language, drug activity, etc.)?
❏ Yes   ❏ No   ❏ Sometimes   Notes _____

Are workers who work late at night or early mornings advised about special precautions to take?
❏ Yes   ❏ No   ❏ Sometimes   Notes _____

Work Environment:
Is there enough lighting to see clearly in all areas where workers must go?
❏ Yes   ❏ No   ❏ Sometimes   Notes _____

Are there safe places for workers to eat, use the restroom, store valuables, etc.?
❏ Yes   ❏ No   ❏ Sometimes   Notes _____

Are there places where workers can go for protection in an emergency?
❏ Yes   ❏ No   ❏ Sometimes   Notes _____

Is safe parking readily available for workers?
❏ Yes   ❏ No   ❏ Sometimes   Notes _____

Security Measures:
Are workers provided two-way radios, pagers or cellular phones?
❏ Yes   ❏ No   ❏ Sometimes   Notes _____

Are workers provided with personal alarm devices or portable panic buttons?
❏ Yes   ❏ No   ❏ Sometimes   Notes _____

Are vehicle door and window locks controlled by the driver?
❏ Yes   ❏ No   ❏ Sometimes   Notes _____

Are vehicles equipped with physical barriers (Plexiglas partitions, etc.)?
❏ Yes   ❏ No   ❏ Sometimes   Notes _____

Work Procedures:
Are workers given maps and good directions covering the areas where they will be working?
❏ Yes   ❏ No   ❏ Sometimes   Notes _____

Are workers given alternative routes to use in neighborhoods with a high crime rate?
❏ Yes   ❏ No   ❏ Sometimes   Notes _____

Does a policy exist to allow workers to refuse service to unruly customers?
❏ Yes   ❏ No   ❏ Sometimes   Notes _____

Has a liaison with the police been established?
☐ Yes   ☐ No   ☐ Sometimes   Notes _____

Do workers avoid carrying unnecessary items, which someone could use as a weapon against them?
☐ Yes   ☐ No   ☐ Sometimes   Notes _____

Is a safe vehicle or other transportation provided by the employer for use when conducting company business?
☐ Yes   ☐ No   ☐ Sometimes   Notes _____

Are vehicles used in the field routinely inspected and kept in good working order?
☐ Yes   ☐ No   ☐ Sometimes   Notes _____

Is there always someone who knows where each worker is while traveling during business hours?
☐ Yes   ☐ No   ☐ Sometimes   Notes _____

Are workers notified of past violent acts committed by customers or other personnel?
☐ Yes   ☐ No   ☐ Sometimes   Notes _____

Are special precautions taken when workers:
Perform "enforcement" functions (parking control officers, inspectors, etc.)?
☐ Yes   ☐ No   ☐ Sometimes   Notes _____

Have to take something away from customers (illegal credit cards)?
☐ Yes   ☐ No   ☐ Sometimes   Notes _____

Have contact with people who behave violently?
☐ Yes   ☐ No   ☐ Sometimes   Notes _____

Have contact with dangerous animals (dogs, rodents, etc.)?
☐ Yes   ☐ No   ☐ Sometimes   Notes _____

OSHA
Occupational Safety and
Health Administration

Appendix B:
Incident Report Forms

Sample Incident Report Form 1:
This incident report was adapted from *Violence on the Job: a Guidebook for Labor and Management,* published by the Labor Occupational Health Program, University of California, Berkeley.

Workplace Violence Incident Report Form

Personal Information

Name (*optional*)_____

☐ Male   ☐ Female

Job title _____

Facility/employer address

_____
_____
_____
_____

Years in current job _____

Incident Description

Date incident occurred _____

Time incident occurred _____

Location where incident occurred (*be specific*)

_____
_____
_____
_____
_____

Describe the incident

_____
_____
_____
_____
_____
_____

Type of incident (*check all that apply*)

- ☐ Grabbed
- ☐ Kicked
- ☐ Hit with object
- ☐ Shot (or attempted)
- ☐ Threatened with weapon
- ☐ Bomb threat
- ☐ Vandalism (employer's property)
- ☐ Arson

- ☐ Pushed
- ☐ Scratched
- ☐ Bitten
- ☐ Sexually assaulted
- ☐ Verbally harassed
- ☐ Animal attack
- ☐ Vandalism (own property)

- ☐ Slapped
- ☐ Hit with fist
- ☐ Knifed (or attempted)
- ☐ Assaulted with weapon
- ☐ Verbally threatened
- ☐ Robbery
- ☐ Other

What type of weapon was used? How was the weapon obtained?

_____
_____
_____
_____
_____

Were you working alone? If no, who was with you that may have witnessed the incident?

_____
_____
_____
_____
_____

Were security personnel on duty at the time of the assault? If yes, was security notified? Did security respond? When?

_____
_____
_____
_____
_____

Who threatened or assaulted you?

- ☐ Client/customer
- ☐ Student
- ☐ Co-worker
- ☐ Passenger
- ☐ Spouse or partner
- ☐ Robber/burglar

- ☐ Patient
- ☐ Family/friend of client or patient
- ☐ Supervisor/manager
- ☐ Person in custody
- ☐ Former spouse or partner

- ☐ Parent
- ☐ Stranger
- ☐ Animal
- ☐ Other

OSHA
Occupational Safety and
Health Administration

Were any threats made before the incident occurred? If yes, did you ever report to your supervisor or manager that you were threatened, harassed or suspicious that the attacker may become violent?

_____
_____
_____
_____

Incident Analysis

❏ Yes ❏ No   Has this type of incident occurred before at the workplace?

What do you think were the main factors that contributed to the incident?

_____
_____
_____
_____

What could have prevented or at least minimized the damage caused by this incident?

_____
_____
_____
_____

Post-Incident Response

❏ Yes ❏ No   Did you require medical attention as a result of the incident?

❏ Yes ❏ No   Did you miss work as a result of the incident?

❏ Yes ❏ No   Did you apply for workers' compensation?

❏ Yes ❏ No   Was the incident reported to a supervisor or manager?

❏ Yes ❏ No   Was a police report filed?

❏ Yes ❏ No   Was immediate counseling provided to affected workers and witnesses who desired it?

❏ Yes ❏ No   Was critical incident debriefing provided to all affected staff who desired it?

❏ Yes ❏ No   Was post-trauma (follow-up) counseling provided to all affected staff who desired it?

❏ Yes ❏ No   Was all counseling provided by a professional counselor?

❏ Yes ❏ No   Was the counseling effective?

❏ Yes ❏ No   Was the victim advised about legal rights?

Report completed by _____

Department/Job Title/Union Position_____

Date _____ Phone number _____

E-mail _____

RECOMMENDATIONS FOR WORKPLACE VIOLENCE PREVENTION PROGRAMS IN
LATE-NIGHT RETAIL ESTABLISHMENTS

Sample Incident Report Form 2:

Reprinted with permission of the Hartford Financial Services Group, Inc., *Workplace Violence Prevention Program Loss Control TIPS—Technical Information Paper Series.*

Victim's Name _____ Job Title _____

Victim's Address _____

Home Phone Number _____ Work Phone Number _____

Employer's Name and Address _____

Department/Section _____

Victim's Social Security Number _____

Incident Date _____

Incident Time _____

Incident Location _____

Work Location (*if different*) _____

Type of Incident: (*check one*) ☐ Assault ☐ Robbery ☐ Harassment ☐ Disorderly Conduct
☐ Sex Offense ☐ Other (*Please Specify*) _____

(*See* **Definition of Incidents Worksheet**)

Were You Injured?　　　　　　　　　☐ Yes　　　　☐ No

If yes, please specify your injuries and the location of any treatment

_____

_____

_____

_____

Did Police Respond to Incident　　　　☐ Yes　　　　☐ No

What Police Department _____

Police Report Filed　　　　　　　　　☐ Yes　　　　☐ No

　　Report Number _____

Was Your Supervisor Notified　　　　　☐ Yes　　　　☐ No

Supervisor's Name _____

Was the Local Union/Employee Representative Notified　　　☐ Yes　　　　☐ No

　　Who should be notified _____

Was Any Action Taken By Employer (specify) _____

_____

Assailant/Perpetrator (*check one*) ☐ Intruder ☐ Customer ☐ Patient ☐ Resident
☐ Client ☐ Visitor ☐ Student ☐ Co-Worker ☐ Former Worker ☐ Supervisor
☐ Family/Friend ☐ Other (*specify*)

_____

21. Assailant/Perpetrator—Name/Address/Age (if known): _____

_____

_____

⊙SHA
Occupational Safety and
Health Administration

Please Briefly Describe the Incident _____

_____

Incident Disposition ❑ No action taken ❑ Arrest ❑ Warning ❑ Suspension
❑ Reprimand ❑ Other (*Please Specify*) _____

Did The Incident Involve A Weapon: ❑ Yes   ❑ No
   Specify_____

Did You Lose Any Workdays: ❑ Yes   ❑ No
   Specify_____

Were You Singled Out Or Was The Violence Directed At More Than One Individual _____

Were You Alone When The Incident Occurred_____

Did You Have Any Reason To Believe Than An Incident
   Might Occur   ❑ Yes   ❑ No
   Why _____

Has This Type Or Similar Incident(s) Happened To You Or Your
   Co-workers: ❑ Yes   ❑ No
   Specify_____

Have You Had Any Counseling Or Support Since The Incident: ❑ Yes   ❑ No
   Specify_____

What Do You Feel Can Be Done In The Future To Avoid Such An Incident _____

Was This Assailant Involved In Previous Incidents _____

Are There Any Measures In Place To Prevent Similar Incidents: ❑ Yes   ❑ No
   Specify_____

Has Corrective Action Been Taken: ❑ Yes   ❑ No
   Specify_____

_____

Comments _____

_____

_____

_____

Definition of Incidents

Assault

The intentional use of physical injury, (impairment of physical condition or substantial pain) to another person, with or without a weapon or dangerous instrument.

Criminal Mischief

Intentional or reckless damaging of the property of another person without permission.

Disorderly Conduct

Intentionally causing public inconvenience, annoyance or alarm or recklessly creating a risk thereof by fighting (without injury) or violent, numinous (mysterious) or threatening behavior or making unreasonable noise, shouting abuse, misbehaving, disturbing an assembly or meeting or persons or creating hazardous conditions by an act which serves no legitimate purpose.

Harassment

Intentionally striking, shoving or kicking another or subjecting another person to physical contact, or threatening to do the same (without physical injury). ALSO, using abusive or obscene language or following a person in/about a public place, or engaging in a course of conduct which alarms or seriously annoys another person.

Larceny

Wrongful taking, depriving or withholding property from another (no force involved). Victim may or may not be present.

Menacing

Intentionally places or attempts to place another person in fear of imminent serious physical injury.

Reckless Endangerment

Subjecting individuals to danger by recklessly engaging in conduct which creates substantial risk of serious physical injury.

Robbery

Forcible stealing of another's property by use of threat or immediate physical force. Victim is present and aware of theft.

Sex Offense

Public Lewdness:	Exposure of sexual organs to others.
Sexual Abuse:	Subjecting another to sexual contact without consent.
Sodomy:	A deviant sexual act committed as in rape.
Rape:	Sexual intercourse without consent.

Workplace Violence Prevention Program © 2008 The Hartford Loss Control Department

OSHA
Occupational Safety and
Health Administration

Appendix C:
States with Workplace Violence Standards

Below are examples of State Plan standards that address workplace violence. If employers maintain businesses in any state plan states they should contact the state occupational safety and
health office to ensure that they have the most current standards.

New Mexico

The New Mexico Environmental Improvement Board, which issues occupational safety and
health standards, issued a regulation (11.5.6) that requires convenience stores open between
the hours of 11 p.m. and 5 a.m. either to have two workers on duty, or one clerk and a security
guard, or to install bulletproof glass or other safety features to limit access to store personnel.
See www.nmenv.state.nm.us/NMED_regs/osha/11nmac5_6.doc for more information.

Washington

Several existing provisions of the Washington Administrative Code (WAC) may apply to the hazards of violence in the workplace. The provision that is specific to late-night retail is: WAC 296-
832, the "Late Night Retail Workers Crime Protection Standard," provides specific violence-related
direction to retail businesses that operate between 11:00 p.m. and 6:00 a.m. Restaurants, hotels,
taverns and lodging facilities are beyond the scope of this rule. See http://lni.wa.gov/Safety/Rules/
Policies/PDFs/WRD505.pdf for more information.

Appendix D:
Bibliography and References

Bibliography

Albence, M.T. (1994). "Convenient Targets: An Examination of Convenience Store Robberies in Carbondale, Illinois, from 1986 to 1993." *Unpublished Master's Thesis,* Southern Illinois University at Carbondale.

Alexander, R.H., Franklin, G.M., and Wolf, M.L. (1994). "The sexual assault of women at work in Washington State, 1980-1989." *American Journal of Public Health* 84 (4):640-642.

Amandus, H.E. (1995). "Reevaluation of the effectiveness of environmental designs to reduce robbery risk in Florida convenience stores." *Journal of Occupational and Environmental Medicine* 37:711-717.

Amandus, H.E. (1995). "Status of NIOSH research on prevention of robbery-related intentional injuries to convenience store workers." *National Institute of Justice Research Report: Trends, Risks, and Interventions in Lethal Violence, Proceedings of Third Annual Spring Symposium of the Homicide Research Working Group,* Atlanta, GA. pp. 217-228.

Amandus, H.E. (1997). "Convenience store robberies in selected metropolitan areas: Risk factors for employees injury." *Journal of Occupational and Environmental Medicine* 39(5): 442-447.

American Insurance Services Group, Inc. (1994). "Workplace Violence: A Prevention Program." New York, NY: American Insurance Services Group, Inc.

ASIS International (2005). *Workplace Violence Prevention and Response Guide.* (http://www.asisonline.org/guidelines/guidelineswpvfinal.pdf).

Askari, E. (1997). "Violence on the Job: A Guidebook for Labor and Management." Berkeley, CA: University of California.

Athena Research Corporation. (1981). "Robber Interview Report." Presented to Crime Committee of the Southland Corporation, Dallas, TX.

Bachman, R. (1994). "Violence and Theft in the Workplace." *National Crime Victimization Survey.* Washington, DC: U.S. Department of Justice, Bureau of Justice Statistics.

Bellamy, L. (1995). "Situational Crime Prevention Strategies for Combating Convenience Store Robbery." Unpublished paper, Rutgers, The State University of New Jersey.

Bellamy, L. (1996). "Situational Crime Prevention and Convenience Stores Robbery." *Security Journal* 7:41-52.

Calder, J.D. and Bauer, J.R. (1992). "Convenience Store Robberies: Security Measures and Store Robbery Incidents." *Journal of Criminal Justice* 20:553-556.

California State Department of Industrial Relations. (1994). *CAL/OSHA Guidelines for Workplace Security.* San Francisco, CA: Division of Occupational Safety and Health.

California State Department of Industrial Relations. (1995). *Model Injury and Illness Prevention Program for Workplace Security.*

Clarke, R.V. (1983) "Situational Crime Prevention: Its theoretical basis and practical scope." *Crime and Justice: An Annual Review of Research* 4:225-256.

Clifton, W., Jr. and Callahan, P.T. (1987) Convenience Store Robberies: An Intervention Strategy by the City of Gainesville; Gainesville, FL: Gainesville Police Department.

Convenience Business Security Act. (1992) Supplement to Florida Statutes 1991. (§§ 812.1701 — 812.1750).

Cook, P.J. (1987). "Robbery Violence." *Journal of Criminal Law & Criminology* 78(2) pp. 357-375.

Crow, W.J. and Bull, J.L. (1975). *Robbery Deterrence: An Applied Behavioral Science Demonstration.* La Jolla, CA: Western Behavioral Sciences Institute.

Crow, W.J., Erickson. R.J., and Scott, L. (1987), "Set Your Sights on Preventing Retail Violence." *Security Management* 31 (9): 60-64.

OSHA
Occupational Safety and
Health Administration

Degner, R.L. et al. (1983), "Food Store Robberies in Florida: Detailed Crime Statistics." Florida Agricultural Market Research Center, Gainesville, FL.

Erickson, R.J. (1991). "Convenience Store Homicide and Rape." In National Association of Convenience Stores (Ed.). *Convenience Store Security*. Alexandria, VA. pp. 29-101.

Erickson, R.J. (1995). "Employer Liability for Workplace Violence." In Fitzpatrick, R. *Tips on Employment Law* 5:1-7. Washington, DC, American Bar Association.

Erickson, R.J. (1996). *Armed Robbers and Their Crimes*. Seattle, WA: Athena Research.

Erickson, R.J. (1996) "Retail Employees as a Group at Risk for Violence." *Occupational Medicines: State of the Art Reviews* 11(2): 269-275.

Erickson, R.J. (1998). *Convenience Store Security at the Millennium*. Alexandria, VA: National Association of Convenience Stores.

Federal Bureau of Investigation (1993). Crimes in the United States: Uniform Crime Reports. Washington, DC: United States Department of Justice.

Figlio, R. and Aurand, S. (1991). "An Assessment of Robbery Deterrence Measures at Convenience Stores." In National Association of Convenience Stores (Ed.). *Convenience Store Security* 103-138. Alexandria, VA. pp. 103-138.

Flannery, R.B., et al. (1991). "A program to help staff cope with psychological sequelae of assaults by patients." *Hospital Community Psychiatry* 42:935-938.

Flannery, R.B., et al. (1994). "Risk Factors for psychiatric inpatient assaults on staff." *Mental Health Administration* 21:24-31.

Flannery, R.B., et al. (1995). "The Assaulted Staff Action Program (ASAP): Guidelines for Fielding a Team." In Vandenbos, G.R. and Bulatao, E.Q. (Eds.). *Violence on the Job* 327-342. Washington, DC: American Psychological Association.

Hales, T., et al. (1988). "Occupational Injuries Due to Violence." *Journal of Occupational and Environmental Medicine* 30(6): 483-487.

Hunter, R.D. (1999). "Convenience Store Robbery Revisited: A Review of Prevention Results." Journal of Security Administration 22(1): pp. 1-14

Hunter, R.D. (1990). "Convenience store robbery in Tallahassee: A Reassessment", FL: Journal of Security Administration.

Hunter, R.D. and Jeffery, C.R. (1991). "Environmental Crime Prevention: An Analysis of Convenience Store Robberies," *Security Journal* 2(2): 78-83.

Jeffery, C.R., Hunter, R.D., and Griswold, J. (1987). "Crime Prevention and Computer Analysis of Convenience Store Robberies in Tallahassee, Florida," *Florida Police Journal* 34: 65-69.

Kinney, J.A., and Johnson, D.L. (1993). *Breaking Point: the Workplace Violence Epidemic and What to Do about It*. Chicago, IL: National Safe Workplace Institute.

Kraus, J.F., Blander, B., and McArthur, D.L. (1995). "Incidence, Risk Factors and Prevention Strategies for Work-related Assault Injuries: A Review of What is Known, What Needs to Be Known, and Countermeasures for Intervention. *Annual Review of Public Health* (16)355-79.

Liberty Mutual (2004). Liberty mutual workplace safety index: the direct costs and leading causes of workplace injuries. Boston, MA: Liberty Mutual, 4 pp. [http://www.libertymutual.com/omapps/ContentServer?cid=1078439448036&pagename=ResearchCenter%2FDocument%2FShowDoc&c=Document].

Matchulat, J.J. (2007). "Separating Fact from Fiction about Workplace Violence." *Employee Relations Law Journal* 33(2) 14-22.

NIOSH (2006). *Workplace Violence Prevention Strategies and Research Needs*. Conference held in Baltimore, Maryland, November 17-19, 2004. Cincinnati, OH: U.S. Department of Health and Human Services, Centers for Disease and Control Prevention, National

Institute for Occupational Safety and Health. DHHS (NIOSH) Publication number 2006-144. [www.cdc.gov/niosh/docs/2006-144]

Northwestern National Life Employee Benefits Division. (1993). *Fear and Violence in the Workplace*. Minneapolis, MN: Northwestern National Life Insurance Company.

Pearson, G.W. (2005). "Controlling the Risk of Violence in the Retail Workplace." *Risk Management*.

Reiss, A.J., Jr., and Roth, J.A. (Eds.). (1993). *Understanding and Preventing Violence*. Washington, DC: National Academy Press.

Rugala, E.A., and Isaacs, A.R. (2004). *Workplace violence: Issues in response*. Quantico, VA: FBI Academy, Federal Bureau of Investigation, National Center for the Analysis of Violent Crime, Critical Incident Response Group [www.fbi.gov/publications/violence.pdf].

Schreiber, B. (1991). "Survey of Convenience Store Crime and Security." Convenience store security: report and recommendations. Alexandria, VA: National Association of Convenience Stores.

Toscano, G. and Weber, W. (1995). Violence in the Workplace. Washington, DC: U.S. Department of Labor, Bureau of Labor Statistics.

Toscano G. and Windau, J. (1994). "The Changing Character of Fatal Work Injuries." *Fatal Workplace Injuries in 1993: A Collection of Data and Analysis* 6-17. Washington, DC: U.S. Department of Labor, Bureau of Labor Statistics.

U.S. Department of Justice. (1994). *Criminal Victimization in the United States*, 1992. Pub. No. NCJ-145 125. Washington, DC.

U.S. Department of Labor, Bureau of Labor Statistics, (1994). Violence in the Workplace Comes Under Closer Scrutiny. Summary 94-10. Washington, DC.

Virginia Crime Prevention Center. (1993). Violent Crimes in Convenience Stores: Analysis of Crimes, Criminals, and Costs. House Document No. 30, Richmond, VA: Commonwealth of Virginia.

Washington Crime News Services. (1994). "New Police Approach Reduces Convenience Store Crime." *Crime Control Digest* 28(1): 1, 4-5.

Workers' Compensation Board of British Columbia. (1995). Take Care: How to Develop and Implement a Workplace Violence Prevention Program (A Guide for Small Business). Vancouver, BC: Workers' Compensation Board of British Columbia.

Zahn, M.A. and Sagi, P.C. (1987). "Stranger Homicides in Nine American Cities." *Journal of Criminal Law & Criminology* 78(2): 377-397.

References

U.S. Department of Justice, Bureau of Justice Statistics. (2001). *National Crime Victimization Survey. Violence in the Workplace*, 1993-99. www.ojp.gov/bjs/pub/pdf/vw99.pdf

U.S. Department of Labor, Bureau of Labor Statistics. (2008). *Census of Fatal Occupational Injuries*, 2006. www.bls.gov/iif/oshwc/cfoi/cftb0215.pdf

U.S. Department of Labor, Bureau of Labor Statistics. (2007). *Survey of Occupational Injuries and Illnesses*, 2006. www.bls.gov/iif/oshwc/osh/case/ostb1796.pdf

U.S. Department of Labor, Bureau of Labor Statistics. (2006). *Survey of Workplace Violence Prevention*, 2005. www.bls.gov/iif/osh_wpvs.htm

OSHA Assistance

OSHA can provide extensive help through a variety of programs, including technical assistance about effective safety and health programs, state plans, workplace consultations, and training and education.

Safety and Health Management System Guidelines

Effective management of worker safety and health protection is a decisive factor in reducing the extent and severity of work-related injuries and illnesses and their related costs. In fact, an effective safety and health management system forms the basis of good worker protection, can save time and money, increase productivity and reduce employee injuries, illnesses and related workers' compensation costs.

To assist employers and workers in developing effective safety and health management systems, OSHA published recommended Safety and Health Program Management Guidelines (54 *Federal Register* (16): 3904-3916, January 26, 1989). These voluntary guidelines can be applied to all places of employment covered by OSHA.

The guidelines identify four general elements critical to the development of a successful safety and health management system:

• Management leadership and worker involvement,
• Worksite analysis,
• Hazard prevention and control, and
• Safety and health training.

The guidelines recommend specific actions, under each of these general elements, to achieve an effective safety and health management system. The *Federal Register* notice is available online at www.osha.gov.

State Programs

The *Occupational Safety and Health Act of 1970* (OSH Act) encourages states to develop and operate their own job safety and health plans. OSHA approves and monitors these plans. Twenty-five states, Puerto Rico and the Virgin Islands currently operate approved state plans: 22 cover both private and public (state and local government) employment; Connecticut, Illinois, New Jersey, New York and the Virgin Islands cover the public sector only. States and territories with their own OSHA-approved occupational safety and health plans must adopt standards identical to, or at least as effective as, the Federal OSHA standards.

Consultation Services

Consultation assistance is available on request to employers who want help in establishing and maintaining a safe and healthful workplace. Largely funded by OSHA, the service is provided at no cost to the employer. Primarily developed for smaller employers with more hazardous operations, the consultation service is delivered by state governments employing professional safety and health consultants. Comprehensive assistance includes an appraisal of all mechanical systems, work practices, and occupational safety and health hazards of the workplace and all aspects of the employer's present job safety and health program. In addition, the service offers assistance to employers in developing and implementing an effective safety and health program. No penalties are proposed or citations issued for hazards identified by the consultant. OSHA provides consultation assistance to the employer with the assurance that his or her name and firm and any information about the workplace will not be routinely reported to OSHA enforcement staff. For more information concerning consultation assistance, see OSHA's website at www.osha.gov.

Strategic Partnership Program

OSHA's Strategic Partnership Program helps encourage, assist and recognize the efforts of partners to eliminate serious workplace hazards and achieve a high level of worker safety and health. Most strategic partnerships seek to have a broad impact by building cooperative relationships with groups of employers and workers. These partnerships are voluntary relationships between OSHA, employers, worker representatives, and others (e.g., trade unions, trade and professional associations, universities, and other government agencies).

For more information on this and other agency programs, contact your nearest OSHA office, or visit OSHA's website at www.osha.gov.

OSHA Training and Education

OSHA area offices offer a variety of information services, such as technical advice, publications, audiovisual aids and speakers for special engagements. OSHA's Training Institute in Arlington Heights, IL, provides basic and advanced courses in safety and health for Federal and state compliance officers, state consultants, Federal agency personnel, and private sector employers, workers and their representatives.

The OSHA Training Institute also has established OSHA Training Institute Education Centers to address the increased demand for its courses from the private sector and from other federal agencies. These centers are colleges, universities, and nonprofit organizations that have been selected after a competition for participation in the program.

OSHA also provides funds to nonprofit organizations, through grants, to conduct workplace training and education in subjects where OSHA believes there is a lack of workplace training. Grants are awarded annually.

For more information on grants, training and education, contact the OSHA Training Institute, Directorate of Training and Education, 2020 South Arlington Heights Road, Arlington Heights, IL 60005, (847) 297-4810, or see Training on OSHA's website at www.osha.gov. For further information on any OSHA program, contact your nearest OSHA regional office listed at the end of this publication.

Information Available Electronically

OSHA has a variety of materials and tools available on its website at www.osha.gov. These include electronic tools, such as *Safety and Health Topics*, *eTools*, *Expert Advisors*; regulations, directives and publications; videos and other information for employers and workers. OSHA's software programs and eTools walk you through challenging safety and health issues and common problems to find the best solutions for your workplace.

OSHA Publications

OSHA has an extensive publications program. For a listing of free items, visit OSHA's website at www.osha.gov or contact the OSHA Publications Office, U.S. Department of Labor, 200 Constitution Avenue, NW, N-3101, Washington, DC 20210; telephone (202) 693-1888 or fax to (202) 693-2498.

Contacting OSHA

To report an emergency, file a complaint, or seek OSHA advice, assistance, or products, call (800) 321-OSHA or contact your nearest OSHA Regional or Area office listed at the end of this publication. The teletypewriter (TTY) number is (877) 889-5627.

Written correspondence can be mailed to the nearest OSHA Regional or Area Office listed at the end of this publication or to OSHA's national office at: U.S. Department of Labor, Occupational Safety and Health Administration, 200 Constitution Avenue, N.W., Washington, DC 20210.

By visiting OSHA's website at www.osha.gov, you can also:
- File a complaint online,
- Submit general inquiries about workplace safety and health electronically, and
- Find more information about OSHA and occupational safety and health.

OSHA
Occupational Safety and
Health Administration

OSHA Regional Offices

Region I
(CT*, ME, MA, NH, RI, VT*)
JFK Federal Building, Room E340
Boston, MA 02203
(617) 565-9860

Region II
(NJ*, NY*, PR*, VI*)
201 Varick Street, Room 670
New York, NY 10014
(212) 337-2378

Region III
(DE, DC, MD*, PA, VA*, WV)
The Curtis Center
170 S. Independence Mall West
Suite 740 West
Philadelphia, PA 19106-3309
(215) 861-4900

Region IV
(AL, FL, GA, KY*, MS, NC*, SC*, TN*)
61 Forsyth Street, SW, Room 6T50
Atlanta, GA 30303
(404) 562-2300

Region V
(IL*, IN*, MI*, MN*, OH, WI)
230 South Dearborn Street
Room 3244
Chicago, IL 60604
(312) 353-2220

Region VI
(AR, LA, NM*, OK, TX)
525 Griffin Street, Room 602
Dallas, TX 75202
(972) 850-4145

Region VII
(IA*, KS, MO, NE)
Two Pershing Square
2300 Main Street, Suite 1010
Kansas City, MO 64108-2416
(816) 283-8745

Region VIII
(CO, MT, ND, SD, UT*, WY*)
1999 Broadway, Suite 1690
PO Box 46550
Denver, CO 80202-5716
(720) 264-6550

Region IX
(AZ*, CA*, HI*, NV*, and American Samoa,
Guam and the Northern Mariana Islands)
90 7th Street, Suite 18-100
San Francisco, CA 94103
(415) 625-2547

Region X
(AK*, ID, OR*, WA*)
1111 Third Avenue, Suite 715
Seattle, WA 98101-3212
(206) 553-5930

* These states and territories operate their own OSHA-approved job safety and health programs and cover state and local government employees as well as private sector employees. The Connecticut, Illinois, New Jersey, New York and Virgin Islands plans cover public employees only. States with approved programs must have standards that are identical to, or at least as effective as, the Federal OSHA standards.

Note: To get contact information for OSHA Area Offices, OSHA-approved State Plans and OSHA Consultation Projects, please visit us online at www.osha.gov or call us at 1-800-321-OSHA.

Endnotes

Chapter 1

[1] All of which can be found at Erika Harrell, *Workplace Violence, 1993-2009: National Crime Victimization Survey and the Census of Fatal Occupational Injuries* (Washington, DC: U.S. Department of Justice, 2011), http://bjs. ojp.usdoj.gov/content/pub/pdf/wv09.pdf.

Chapter 2

[1] Society for Human Resource Management, "Criminal Records/Back ground Checking Laws," http://www.shrm.org/LegalIssues/Stateand LocalResources/StateandLocalStatutesandRegulations/Documents/ Criminalandbackground%20checks.pdf.

[2] Federal Trade Commission, "Fair Credit Reporting Act," http://www. ftc.gov/enforcement/statutes/fair-credit-reporting-act.

[3] U.S. Equal Employment Opportunity Commission, *EEOC Enforcement Guidance: Consideration of Arrest and Conviction Records in Employment Decisions under Title VII of the Civil Rights Act of 1964*, 4/25/2012, http:// www.eeoc.gov/laws/guidance/arrest_conviction.cfm.

[4] The Final Rule was published in the *Federal Register* on September 24, 2013, and became effective on March 24, 2014. However, contractors with a written affirmative action program (AAP) already in place on the effective date have additional time to come into compliance with the AAP requirements. The compliance structure of the Final Rule seeks to provide contractors the opportunity to maintain their current AAP cycle. A link to the Office of Federal Contract Compliance Program's FAQ page can be found at http://www.dol.gov/ofccp/regs/ compliance/vevraa.htm.

[5] U.S. Office of Personnel Management, "Assessment & Selection: Other Assessment Methods: Integrity/Honesty Tests," http://www. opm.gov/policy-data-oversight/assessment-and-selection/other-assessment-methods/integrityhonesty-tests/.

[6] U.S. Equal Employment Opportunity Commission, "Informal Discussion Letter: Title VII and the ADA: Integrity Tests," September 9, 2013, http://www.eeoc.gov/eeoc/foia/letters/2013/title_vii_ada_integrity_tests.html.

Chapter 3

[1] Occupational Safety and Health Administration, "OSH Act of 1970—Sec. 5. Duties," https://www.osha.gov/pls/oshaweb/owadisp.show_document?p_id=3359&p_table=oshact.

[2] Occupational Safety & Health Administration, "Standard Interpretations—Table of Contents: Interpretation Letter," February 9, 2009, https://www.osha.gov/pls/oshaweb/owadisp.show_document?p_table=INTERPRETATIONS&p_id=27406.

[3] Occupational Safety and Health Administration, "Enforcement Procedures for Investigating or Inspecting Incidents of Workplace Violence," September 8, 2011, https://www.osha.gov/OshDoc/Directive_pdf/CPL_02-01-052.pdf.

[4] Society for Human Resources, "Domestic & Workplace Violence/Crime Victims/Weapons Laws," January 2014, http://www.shrm.org/LegalIssues/StateandLocalResources/StateandLocalStatutesandRegulations/Documents/Weaponsviolencelaws.pdf.

[5] *Mitchell v. University of Kentucky, Ky.*, No. 10-CI-00489, 4/26/12.

[6] Kentucky Legislature, Revised Statute KRS Chapter 237.115(1): "Prohibition by local government units of carrying concealed deadly weapons in governmental buildings—Restriction on criminal penalties," http://www.lrc.ky.gov/Statutes/statute.aspx?id=11133.

[7] The difference between the term "weapon" ("something used to injure, defeat, or destroy"—see http://www.merriam-webster.com/dictionary/weapon), and "deadly weapon," as defined in the chapter, is the actual use to which the instrument is put. The term "deadly weapon" has been defined in numerous ways in cases, legal dictionaries, and online free reference publications. The definitions generally include two elements: first, a broad definition (for example, "an instrument, substance, or device, which is used or intended to be used in a way that is likely to cause death") that could encompass work tools, cars, and even—according to one court decision—body parts; and a second, more specific phrase related to instruments that by themselves are likely to

cause death, such as a gun, regardless of the user's intent. Any definition in a company's weapons policy should include both elements.

Chapter 4

[1] The Workplace Bullying Institute website is available at http://www.workplacebullying.org.

[2] Gary Namie, "Workplace Bullying: Escalated Incivility," *Ivey Business Journal*, November/December 2003, http://www.workplacebullying.org/multi/pdf/N-N-2003A.pdf.

[3] Although workplace bullying can include bullying by an individual outside the company (for example, vendor, customer, client), the most frequent circumstance involves an employee-bully and an employee-victim. That is the scenario with which this chapter deals.

[4] Teresa A. Daniel, *Stop Bullying at Work: Strategies and Tools for HR and Legal* Professionals (Alexandria, VA: Society for Human Resource Management, 2009), p. 14.

[5] Daniel, *Stop Bullying at Work*, p. 15.

[6] Reza Emdad, Akbar Alipour, Jan Hagberg, & Irene B. Jensen, "The Impact of Bystanding to Workplace Bullying on Symptoms of Depression among Women and Men in Industry in Sweden: An Empirical and Theoretical Longitudinal Study," *International Archives of Occupational & Environmental Health*, 86, no. 6 (2013): 709-716: doi: 10.1007/s00420-012-0813-1. The report is available for open access at Springerlink.com.

[7] The WorkSafe SmartMove website is available at http://smartmove.safetyline.wa.gov.au/.

[8] Occupational Safety and Health Administration, "Enforcement Procedures for Investigating or Inspecting Incidents of Workplace Violence," September 8, 2011, https://www.osha.gov/OshDoc/Directive_pdf/CPL_02-01-052.pdf.

[9] The Healthy Workplace Bill website is available at http://www.healthyworkplacebill.org.

[10] Florida, Hawaii, Massachusetts, New Hampshire, New Mexico, New York, Pennsylvania, West Virginia, Wisconsin, and Vermont.

[11] Robert W. Fuller, *Somebodies and Nobodies: Overcoming the Abuse of Rank* (Gabriola Island, Canada: New Society Publishers, 2003).

[12] Occupational Safety and Health Administration, *OSHA Field Safety and Health Manual*, 2011, https://www.osha.gov/OshDoc/Directive_pdf/ADM_04-00-001.pdf.

[13] U.S. Department of Labor, "DOL Workplace Violence Program," n.d., http://www.dol.gov/oasam/hrc/policies/dol-workplace-violence-program.htm.

[14] Angela Johnson Meadows, "Diversity Training: There's an App for That," Diversity Best Practices, November 8, 2011, http://www.diversitybestpractices.com/news-articles/diversity-training-theres-an-app-for-that.

[15] Janice Harper, "Mobbing in the Workplace: Even the Good Go Bad," *Huffington Post*, November 23, 2011, http://www.huffingtonpost.com/janice-harper/mobbing-in-the-workplace-_b_1102815.html.

Chapter 5

[1] ASIS International/Society for Human Resource Management, *Workplace Violence Prevention and Intervention*, 2011, http://www.shrm.org/HRStandards/Documents/WVPI%20STD.pdf.

[2] A copy of the Recommendations, consisting of fewer than 13 pages of actual text and over 20 pages of useful appendices, is included in this book as an appendix. It is also available at Occupational Safety and Health Administration, *Recommendations for Workplace Violence Prevention Programs in Late-Night Retail Establishments*, 2009, OSHA 3153-12R, https://www.osha.gov/Publications/osha3153.pdf.

[3] Occupational Safety and Health Administration, "Enforcement Procedures for Investigating or Inspecting Incidents of Workplace Violence," September 8, 2011, https://www.osha.gov/OshDoc/Directive_pdf/CPL_02-01-052.pdf.

[4] The Kilmann Diagnostics website is available at http://www.kilmanndiagnostics.com.

Chapter 6

[1] Federal Bureau of Investigation, *Workplace Violence: Issues in Response*, 2004, http://www.fbi.gov/stats-services/publications/workplace-violence.

[2] The Centers for Disease Control and Prevention Intimate Partner Violence website is available at http://www.cdc.gov/ViolencePrevention/intimatepartnerviolence/index.html.

[3] Dennis A. Davis, *Threats Pending, Fuses Burning: Managing Workplace Violence* (Palo Alto, Calif.: Davies-Black, 1997), Chapter 2.

Chapter 7

[1] The Corporate Alliance to End Partner Violence website is available at http://www.caepv.org. Cited in *Corporate Alliance to End Partner Violence*, March 1, 2005.

[2] Northeastern University, Center for Criminal Justice Policy Research, *Workplace Violence: Wakefield Responds*, 2004, https://greenleaf.org/wp-content/uploads/2013/11/workplaceviolencereport.pdf.

[3] Dennis A. Davis, *Threats Pending, Fuses Burning: Managing Workplace Violence* (Palo Alto, Calif.: Davies-Black, 1997).

[4] Federal Bureau of Investigation, *Workplace Violence: Issues in Response*, 2004, http://www.fbi.gov/stats-services/publications/workplace-violence.

Chapter 8

[1] Federal Bureau of Investigation, *Workplace Violence: Issues in Response*, 2004, 50, http://www.fbi.gov/stats-services/publications/workplace-violence.

[2] Liberty Mutual Research Institute for Safety, *2012 Liberty Mutual Workplace Safety Index*, 2012, http://www.libertymutualgroup.com/omapps/ContentServer?c=cms_document&pagename=LMGResearchInstitute%2Fcms_document%2FShowDoc&cid=1138365240689.

Chapter 9

[1] *Brownfield v. City of Yakima*, No. 09-35628 (9th Cir. Jul. 27, 2010).

[2] U.S. Equal Employment Opportunity Commission, "Questions and Answers: The Application of Title VII and the ADA to Applicants or Employees Who Experience Domestic or Dating Violence, Sexual Assault, or Stalking," http://www.eeoc.gov/eeoc/publications/qa_domestic_violence.cfm.

Chapter 10

[1] Commonwealth of Pennsylvania, Office of Administration, *An Agency Guide to Workplace Violence Prevention and Response*, 2002, http://www.portal.state.pa.us/portal/server.pt/gateway/PTARGS_0_2_785_716_0_43/http%3B/pubcontent.state.pa.us/publishedcontent/publish/global/files/manuals/m505_6.pdf.

Chapter 11

[1] Commonwealth of Pennsylvania, Office of Administration, *An Agency Guide to Workplace Violence Prevention and Response*, 2002, http://www.portal.state.pa.us/portal/server.pt/gateway/PTARGS_0_2_785_716_0_43/http%3B/pubcontent.state.pa.us/publishedcontent/publish/global/files/manuals/m505_6.pdf.

[2] Ibid.

[3] Ibid.

[4] Dennis Davis, "The Aftermath of Violence and Aggression," (n.d.), http://www.workplaceviolence911.com/docs/AftermathManaging_Crises.pdf.

[5] Ibid.

Index

About the Author

Maria Greco Danaher is a shareholder at the Pittsburgh, Pennsylvania office of Ogletree Deakins law firm. She specializes in representing management in labor relations and employment litigation, and in training, counseling, and advising HR departments and corporate management on these topics. Maria is also a presenter for Pennsylvania Bar Institute continuing legal education programs, and is an adjunct professor for the University of Pittsburgh School of Law, and has been named one of the *"Best Lawyers in America."* She holds a 4th degree Black Belt in the martial art of Tang Soo Do.

About Ogletree Deakins

Ogletree Deakins is one of the largest labor and employment law firms representing management in all types of employment-related legal matters. The firm has over 700 lawyers located in 45 offices across the United States and in Europe.

Ogletree Deakins is the "Law Firm of the Year" in both the Employment Law—Management and Labor Law—Management categories in the 2014 edition of the *U.S. News—Best Lawyers*® "Best Law Firms" list.

Ogletree Deakins was awarded the Starbucks Law & Corporate Affairs Excellence in Diversity Award for 2013. This award recognizes the diversity efforts of Ogletree Deakins, including diversity metrics within the firm's lawyer population, participation in professional diversity events, pipeline support, retention, organizational structure to support diversity, and overall commitment to diversity.

In addition to handling labor and employment law matters, the firm has thriving practices focused on business immigration, employee benefits, and workplace safety and health law. Ogletree Deakins represents a diverse range of clients, from small businesses to *Fortune* 50 companies. To learn more, visit http://www.ogletreedeakins.com.

Additional SHRM-Published Books